大展好書　好書大展
品嘗好書　冠群可期

大展好書　好書大展
品嘗好書　冠群可期

中英文對照武學①

李壽堂 編著　　張連友 校訂

24式

太極拳

學與練

中英文對照
附VCD

大展出版社有限公司

24式太極拳學與練
Study and Practice of 24-form Taiji Quan

作者　李壽堂
Writer　　Shoutang　Li

翻譯者　北美意源書社
孫慧敏　姜淑霞

Translator　　Huimin Sun,　Yiyuan Martial Arts Books. North America

Shuxia Jiang, Yiyuan Martial Arts Books, North America

作者李壽堂和張連友的練功照

弓心伶演示的24式太極拳

前　言

　　24式太極拳是原國家體育運動委員會於1956年組織武術界老前輩和有關專家,在楊氏太極拳的基礎上,按照由簡到繁、由易到難的原則進行改編、整理的,並定名爲「簡化太極拳」。因其由24個動作組成,人們習慣上稱其爲「24式太極拳」。

　　這個套路中去掉了原傳統套路中過多的重複拳勢動作,集中了傳統套路中的主要結構和技術內容,並增加了右式拳勢動作,克服了傳統套路中右勢動作較少的缺點,方便群眾掌握,易學易懂,更有益於群眾健身。

　　太極拳不僅是一種具有攻防作用的武術,而且是一種重要的健身和預防疾病的運動項目。實踐證明,它對人體的神經系統、呼吸循環系統、消化系統和骨骼、肌肉、關節疾病的預防和治療都有著神奇的作用。

　　24式太極拳自創編以來,由於其保留了楊氏太極拳緩慢柔和、連綿不斷、舒展大方、勁力內涵的特點和顯著的健身祛病效果,博得了世人的青睞。目前全世界已有150多個國家和地區,十幾億人學練24式太極

拳。在國內現存的130多個武術拳術，幾千個武術套路中，24式太極拳習練人數最多，流傳地域最廣。爲弘揚太極文化，促進全民健身，造福人類，本書將24式太極拳套路分段逐式精解，以幫助太極拳愛好者自學。

Preface

Under the organization of the Chinese Sports Committee, masters and experts of Wushu created the 「24-form Taiji Quan」in 1957, also known as Simplified Taiji. Based on the Yang style of Taiji, the entire set is composed of simple movements that gradually become more complex.

In 24-form Taiji Quan, many repeated moves in the original routine were removed and the main structure and skill content are strengthened. The movements involving the right side of the body have been added to provide symmetry not found in the old sets. Therefore, it is easier to understand, easier to learn, and more practical to train for fitness.

Taiji is not only a martial art for defense and offense, but also a useful sport for bodybuilding and preventing disease. Studies around the world have shown that long-term Taiji practice provides wondrous effects in preventing and alleviating various diseases in the nervous, respiratory, digestive, circulatory and other systems.

The 24-form Taiji Quan retains the main features of Yang style Taiji, including the slow, continuous, and reaching movements that are soft but full of internal power, and which play an active part in health preservation. Since its development in 1957, around one billion people throughout 150 countries and areas in the world now practice the 24-form Taiji Quan. Of the 130 types of Wushu boxing techniques and the thousands of existing Wushu sets, 24-form Taiji Quan is the only one being practiced by the greatest number of people in farreaching places. This book promotes Taiji culture and its benefits to people all over the world, by presenting clearly the 24-form Taiji Quan step by step. Accordingly, the book assists Taiji enthusiasts to learn the basic movements.

目　錄

Content

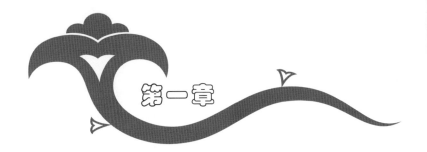

第一章

24式太極拳的基本技術

Chapter 1 Basic Skills of
24-form Taiji Quan

第一節　椿　功

Section 1　Stance Exercises

　　椿功，亦叫站椿，是我國傳統武術特有的練功手段，各流派都非常重視站椿的功法練習，而且各有其獨特的練法。太極拳講究以意行拳，要將意念與拳勢動作完善地結合起來，透過站椿達到調身、調息、調心的功效，並增強下肢功力，使膝關節得到鍛鍊。凡欲在太極拳的功力和健身祛病方面有所收穫者，都應重視站椿的練習，在站椿上下工夫。這裏就太極拳通常採用的幾種站椿功法介紹如下。

Standing Practice (Zhuang Gong, also called Zhan Zhuang) is unique to China's traditional martial arts. Each school emphasizes standing exercises, and each developed their own practicing methods. Taiji Quan movements must be coordinated with the mind. This way of exercising adjusts the whole body, breathing and the heart rate. Practice will enhance the lower half of body and the knee joints in particular. To advance skill and fitness with Taiji Quan, you greatly benefit practicing standing exercises a lot and with consistency and intention. Some commonly used methods are described below.

一、抱球樁（圖1-1、圖1-2）

1. 兩腳平行分開，與肩同寬，自然站立，兩膝微屈，重心落於兩腿中間，使百會穴、會陰穴和兩腳間距中點在一條垂直線上。鬆肩，鬆腰，鬆胯，全身鬆靜，意念集中，無雜念，呼吸自然。

1. Ball-Holding Stance (Bao Qiu Zhuang)（Figure 1-1，Figure 1-2）

（1）Separate the feet so that they are parallel and at shoulder width. Stand naturally，bend knees slightly，and share

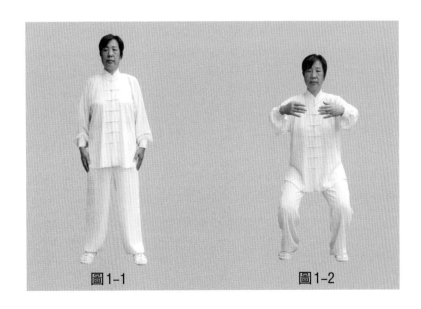

圖1-1　　　　圖1-2

the weight between both legs. Face straight ahead, so that the entire body is aligned vertically. The shoulder, waist, and hip should all be relaxed. The whole body is peaceful; the mind is focused. Breathe naturally.

2. 兩臂慢慢前平舉，微屈，相抱於胸前，手指自然舒展，掌心向內，指尖相對，指尖相距10～20公分。

(2) Raise arms slowly to shoulder level. Stretch fingers naturally. The palms should face each other, as if holding a ball. The hands should be about 10–20cm apart.

3. 兩腿半屈蹲，上體保持正直，眼平視前方。

(3) Bend legs in a half squat, keeping the upper body upright and eyes looking ahead.

【要領】

（1）虛領頂勁，含胸拔背，鬆腰豎脊，沉肩墜肘，圓臂舒指，收腹斂臀，氣沉丹田，全身鬆而不懈，實而不僵。

（2）時間長短因人而異，隨功力的增長，逐漸延長時間，初練時每次站3～5分鐘即可。

Key Points

(1) Neck and head are upright as if holding up something very light. Stand with chest slightly in, shoulders and elbows slightly out, rounded hips and rounded arms. The fingers are relaxed. Inhale through to the abdomen. Maintain an upright but relaxed posture in the whole body.

(2) How long the standing exercises are maintained depends on the individual. As ability and skill improve, increase the practicing time gradually. Beginners might give 3–5 minutes a try.

二、開合椿 (圖1–3、圖1–4、圖1–5)

1. 與抱球椿動作1相同。

2. Open / Close Stance (Kai / he Zhuang) (Figure 1–3, Figure 1–4, Figure 1–5)

(1) Repeat Ball–Holding Stance (1).

2. 在抱球椿的基礎上，兩臂慢慢向外掤開。同時，下肢屈膝下蹲，並做深度吸氣。

(2) Push both arms outward. At the same time, bend the knees lower and breathe deeper.

3. 稍停，兩臂再慢慢收合。同時，兩腿自然站

立，並呼氣。

（3）Pause and close arms gradually. At the same time, stand up and breathe naturally.

【要領】

（1）兩臂外掤時，如抱著個大氣球在充氣，兩臂意在隨氣球增大四面脹出，外掤與吸氣同步。

（2）兩臂收合時，如兩臂要把氣球中的氣擠出，隨氣球縮小，兩臂收合，並同步呼氣。

（3）此開合椿宜用順式呼吸，力求通暢順遂，不可憋氣，隨練習時間的增加，逐步延長開合時間，加深呼吸深度。

圖1-3　　　　　圖1-4　　　　　圖1-5

Key Points

（1）Open arms as if holding an inflating balloon. As the balloon gets bigger, the arms move farther apart. As arms move apart, inhale.

（2）Close arms as if squeezing out the balloon's air. As the arms move closer together, exhale.

（3）Always breathe naturally. Do not hold breath. As practicing time increases, gradually slow down the opening/closing and breathe deeper.

三、升降樁（圖 1-6、圖 1-7、圖 1-8）

1. 與抱球樁動作 1 相同。

3. Rise / Fall Stance（Sheng / Jiang Zhuang）（Figure 1-6, Figure 1-7, Figure 1-8）

（1）Repeat Ball-Holding Stance（1）.

2. 兩臂徐徐前平舉，與肩同高、同寬，手心向下，肘微屈，肩要放鬆。

（2）Raise the arms slowly to shoulder level and maintain the same distance between them. The palms face down; elbows are slightly bent. Relax shoulders.

3. 稍停，兩腿屈膝下蹲。兩掌隨之向下輕輕按至

腹前，停頓片刻，兩腿慢慢站立，兩臂隨之升起。如此循環，次數因人而異，隨功力的增長增加練習次數。

（3）Pause, and then bend legs slowly to half-squat. Lower palms gently until they reach the level of the abdomen. Pause again then slowly straighten the legs. Arms follow the lead and move back to shoulder level. Repeat according to the ability of the individual. Increase repetitions as ability improves.

4. 收功時，兩臂徐徐下落收至大腿兩側，兩腳併攏。

（4）Finish the exercise by slowly moving the arms down to the side of the legs. Place the feet close together.

圖1-6　　　　圖1-7　　　　圖1-8

【要領】

（1）升降時上體保持正直，不可前俯後仰。兩掌下按時，兩肩放鬆前送，兩肘墜沉，兩手如將水中木板下按。上升時，不可聳肩，以肩催肘，肘催腕，腕推掌，向前送勁，與腰背形成對撐。

（2）身體下降後，可隨功力的增強逐漸延長停頓時間。

Key Points

（1）Maintain the upper body straight. Do not bend forward or backward. While pushing the palms down, keep the shoulders relaxed and let the elbows sink as if pressing wood into water. As the body rises, do not raise shoulders. Shoulders lead elbows, elbows lead wrists, and wrists lead the palms. Palms push forward in delivering the energy and the back moves in the opposite direction.

（2）If ability allows, stay in the lower position for a longer period of time.

四、虛步樁（圖1-9）

兩腳併步站立，兩臂自然下垂，右腳尖向右打開，重心徐徐移至右腳並屈膝半蹲，左腳向前邁出半步，腳跟著地，腳尖蹺起，膝微屈。同時，兩手向前上方舉起，在體前合抱，左掌心向右偏下，指與鼻同

高，指尖斜向前上；右掌在左肘內側下方，掌心向左偏下，指尖斜向前上，目視左掌。

左右式交替練習，動作相反。

4. Empty Step Stance (Xu Bu zhuang) (Figure 1-9)

Stand with feet together, arms hanging naturally. Then, move the right foot so that the toes point outwards. The heel still remains in the same position. Shift the weight slowly to the right foot. Bend the right knee. Move the left foot forward in a half step with toes lifted and knee bent. At the same time, raise the left hand to the level of the nose, palm facing the lower right and fingers pointing to the upper front diagonally. The right hand should be a short distance from the left elbow, and the fingertips are at the elbow level. The palm faces lower left

圖1-9

and fingers point upper front. Eyes look at the left hand.

Practice it in the opposite direction.

【要領】

（1）兩腿虛實分明，收腹斂臀，實腿要屈膝，穩固支撐身體；虛腿膝部微屈，不可挺直，腳跟輕輕支撐。

（2）上體保持中正安舒；兩臂要沉肩墜肘，舒指坐腕，勁貫指尖；頭部要虛領頂勁，心念集中。

以上各種椿功練習完畢均要走動遛腿，不宜大聲說話，以增加養功效果。

Key Points

（1）Two legs should be placed differently. One leg should be solidly planted on the ground, supporting the body, knee bent. The other leg, also bent, should be lightly placed on the ground and should support the body gently. Hold in the abdomen and pull the hips in.

（2）Maintain a straight and comfortable upper body. Sink the shoulders and elbows. Keep palm and fingers relaxed. Deliver the energy to the fingertips. Maintain head upright and relaxed. The mind is focused.

After exercises, walk a little to relax legs. To increase power effectively, talk sparingly, and in a gentle voice.

第二節　體　姿
Section 2　Body Positions

現將24式太極拳中出現的主要體姿介紹如下。

The main body positions in 24-form Taiji Quan are described below.

一、手　型

1. 拳

五指蜷曲，拇指壓於食指、中指第二指節上。握拳不可太緊，拳面要平（圖1-10）。

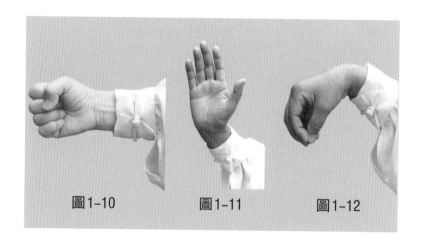

圖1-10　　　　圖1-11　　　　圖1-12

1. Hand Positions

(1) Fist (Quan)

Curl the fingers in, thumb pressing the second section of the index finger and middle finger. Do not hold the fist too tightly or too loosely (Figure 1-10).

2. 掌

五指自然舒展，掌心微合，虎口呈弧形（圖1-11）。

(2) Palm (Zhang)

Stretch five fingers naturally. The「Tiger Mouth」forms an arc. (「Tiger Mouth」is where the thumb and index finger are joined) (Figure 1-11).

3. 勾

五指第一節自然捏攏，屈腕（圖1-12）。

(3) Hook (Gou)

Pinch five fingertips together naturally, bending the wrist down (Figure 1-12).

二、步　型

1. 弓　步

前腿全腳著地，屈膝前弓，膝部不得超過腳尖；

另一腿自然伸直，腳尖內扣斜前方約45°，兩腳橫向距離為10～20公分（圖1-13）。

2. Foot Positions

(1) Bow Step (Gong Bu)

One foot takes a big step and the entire foot is planted on the ground, knee bent. The knee should not be over or past the toes. Straighten the other leg, toes pointing at about 45° outwards, in relation to the body. Feet are on two parallel lines, which distance is about 10 to 20 cm (Figure 1-13).

2. 虛　步

一腿屈膝半蹲，全腳著地，腳尖斜朝前；另一腿微屈，腳前掌或腳跟點地（圖1-14a、圖1-14b）。

(2) Empty Step (Xu Bu)

Bend one knee with the whole foot planted on the ground, toes pointing a little outward. Bend the other knee slightly with

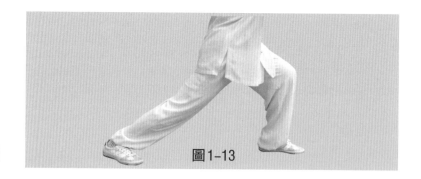

圖1-13

either the palm or the heel of the foot on the ground（Figure 1–14a, Figure 1–14b）.

3. 仆　步

　　一腿全蹲，膝與腳尖稍外撇；另一腿自然伸直，平鋪接近地面，腳尖內扣，兩腳均全腳著地（圖1–15）。

(3) Crouch Stance（Pu Bu）

Squat with one leg and knee and toes slightly point out-

圖1–14a　　　　　　圖1–14b

圖1–15

wards. Extend the whole length of the other leg close to the ground, toes towards inside. The centre of gravity should be low and close to the ground. Both feet are fully placed on the ground (Figure 1–15).

4. 獨立步

一腿自然直立，另一腿屈膝提起，大腿高於水準（圖1-16）。

(4) One Leg Stand (Du Li Bu)

One leg stands while the other one lifted with the knee bent in front of the body. The foot should be placed in front of the standing leg's knee (Figure 1–16).

5. 平行步

兩腳分開，腳尖朝前，屈膝下蹲或自然直立，兩

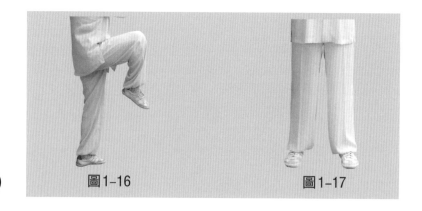

圖1-16   圖1-17

脚外緣同肩寬（圖1-17）。

(5) Parallel Step（Ping Xing Bu）

Place feet apart at shoulder width, toes point forwards. Knees maybe be bent or straightened（Figure 1-17）.

以上幾種步型配合上體中正，均可作為樁功練習。

All the positions above can be used as stance practice with an upright upper body.

三、手　法

1. 拳　法

（1）沖　拳

拳自腰立拳向前打出，高不過肩，低不過胸，力達拳面（見轉身搬攔捶）（圖1-18）。

3. Hand Movements

（1）Fist movements

a. Punch（Chong Quan）

Punch forward, moving the fist from the lower back to shoulder height, turning it at the same time. The fist is no lower than the chest. Force should go to the face of the fist（See 「Turn, Deflect, Parry and Punch」）（Figure 1-18）.

(2)貫　拳

兩拳自下經上體兩側，臂內旋向前上圈貫，與耳同高，拳眼斜向下，兩臂呈弧形（見「雙峰貫耳」）（圖1-19）。

b. Strike with Both Fist(Guan Quan)

Start with arms tucked in at either sides of the body, bent, fists punching forward. The two fists move outwards so that both arms are outstretched on either side. Fists are then brought in to the opponent's ears, eyes of the fists facing 45° down, arms are in arc (See Striking Ears with Both Fists) (Figure 1–19).

2. 掌　法

(1)推　掌

掌須經耳旁，臂內旋向前立掌推出，掌指高不過

圖1-18　　　　　　　　　　圖1-19

眼，力達掌根（見「摟膝拗步」）。

(2) Palm Practice

a. Push（Tui Zhang）

One palm at a time pushes out and forwards from the side of the head. Fingers should not be higher than the eyes. Deliver energy to the base of palms(See「Brush Knee and Twist Steps」).

(2)摟　掌

掌自異側經體前弧形下摟至膝外側，掌心朝下，掌指向前（見「摟膝拗步」）。

b. Brush Hand（Lou Zhang）

Move one hand across from the other side of the body to the outside of the knee on the same side as the hand. The palm is facing downward, fingers pointing forward (See「Brush Knee and Twist Steps」).

(3)攔　掌

掌經體側向上，立掌向胸前攔，掌心朝異側，掌指向上（見「轉身搬攔捶」）。

c. Blocking Hands（Lan Zhang）

Move palm from opposite side of the body upward, stopping in front of the chest. The palm is facing the opposite side, fingers pointing up (See「Turn, Deflect, Parry and Punch」).

(4)平分掌

屈臂，兩掌交叉於胸前，兩臂內旋經面前弧形向左右分開，兩掌高與耳平，兩掌心朝外，掌指向上（見「左（右）蹬腳」）。

d. Separate Palms Evenly (Ping Fen Zhang)

Bend both arms and place them crossed in an 「X」 in front of the body. Turn palms outwards and separate arms out and sideways, stopping when palms are at ear level. Palms are facing outward, fingers pointing up (See 「Kicking with the Right Heel」).

(5)斜分掌

兩手交叉或相抱，斜向上下或前後分開（見「野馬分鬃」和「左（右）攬雀尾」掤式）。

e. Separate Palms Diagonally (Xie Fen Zhang)

Make an 'X' with both arms in front of the body. Separate them, one moving up and another moving down, or one forward and another backward (See 「Splitting the Wild Horse's Mane on Both Sides」 and 「Grasping Bird's Tail」).

(6)雲　掌

兩掌在體前上下交替呈立圓運轉（見「雲手」）。

f. Cloud Hands（Yun Zhang）

Two hands draw large circles in front of the body（See 「Cloud Hands」）.

（7）穿　掌

側掌或平掌沿體前、臂、腿穿伸，指尖與穿伸方向相同，力達指尖（見「左（右）下勢獨立」和「右蹬腳」第一動）。

g. Thrust Hand（Chuan Zhang）

Move a palm along the body, arm, and then leg. The thumb should point up, palm facing up or facing down, depending on the requirements. Deliver the energy to the fingertips（See 「Push Down and Stand on the Left Foot」 and 「Kicking with the Right Foot」 first move）.

（8）架　掌

手臂內旋，掌自下向前上架至頭側上方，臂呈弧形，掌心朝外，掌高過頭（見「左（右）穿梭」）。

h. Upper Block with Palms（Jia Zhang）

Turn palm outward and move it up to the upper side of the head. The arm is arched（See the 「Working with a Shuttle–Left and Right」）.

(9)抱　掌

兩掌合抱，兩臂保持弧形，兩腋須留有空隙（見「野馬分鬃」、「左（右）穿梭」、「左（右）攬雀尾」）。

i. Fist Hold (Bao Zhang)

Two hands are held together, arms are maintained in an arc. All parts of the arms should remain a short distance from the body(See「Splitting the Wild Horse's Mane」,「Working with a Shuttle－Left and Right」,「Grasping Bird's Tail」).

(10)插　掌

手自上向前弧形下插，臂自然伸直，掌指朝斜前下方（見「海底針」）。

j. Palm Thrust (Cha Zhang)

Move the hand forward in arc. Extend the arm naturally, fingers pointing down the front of the body (See「Needle at the Bottom of the Sea」).

(11)掤

屈臂呈弧形舉於體前，掌心朝內，力達前臂外側（見「左（右）攬雀尾」掤式）

k. Forearm Push (Peng)

Bend the arm in front of the body. Push it outward and deliver the energy to the outside of the forearm (See「Grasping Bird's Tail」)

(12)捋

臂呈弧形，單手或雙手向左或右側後捋，臂須外旋或內旋，動作走弧形（見「左（右）攬雀尾」捋式）。

l. Pulling with Two Hands (Lu)

Move one or both hands backward, to the left or the right side, as if pulling something back. Arms move in an arc (See「Grasping Bird's Tail」).

(13)擠

一臂屈於胸前，另一手扶於屈臂手的腕部，或前臂內側，兩臂同時前擠，臂撐圓，高不過肩（見「左（右）攬雀尾」擠式）。

m. Push with Arm and Hand (Ji)

Bend an arm in front of the body. Place the other hand on the wrist or inside of the forearm of the bent arm. Push both the arm and the hand forward at the same time. Arms are bent in a curve no higher than the shoulder (See「Grasping Bird's Tail」).

(14)按

單掌或雙掌自上而下為下按，自後經下向前弧形推出為前按（見「左（右）攬雀尾」按式和「如封似閉」）。

n. Press（An）

Push one or both palms down. This is called 「press down」. Push one or both palms upward and forward. This is called 「press forward」(See 「Grasping Bird's Tail」, 「Apparent Close」).

四、步 法

1. 上 步

一腿支撐，另一腿提起經支撐腿內側向前上步，腳跟先著地，隨著重心前移，全腳著地（見「左（右）野馬分鬃」和「左（右）摟膝拗步」）。

4. Steps

(1) Forward Step (Shang Bu)

One leg supports the body. Lift the other foot from the inside of the supporting leg and move it forward, placing the heel to the floor first. As the weight is shifted, place the entire foot on the floor and the leg becomes the supporting leg (See 「Splitting the Wild Horse's Mane」 and 「Brush Knee and Twist Steps」).

2. 退　步

一腿支撐，另一腿經支撐腿內側退一步，腳前掌先著地，隨著重心後移，全腳著地（見「左（右）倒捲肱」）。

(2) Backward Step (Tui Bu)

One leg supports the body. Lift the other foot from the inside of the supporting leg and move it backward, placing the heel to the floor first. As the weight is shifted, place the entire foot on the floor and the leg becomes the supporting leg (See 「Backward Steps and Swirling Arms」).

3. 側行步

一腿支撐，另一腿提起側向開步，腳前掌先著地，隨著重心橫移，全腳著地逐漸過渡為支撐腿；另一腿提起，向支撐腿內側併步，仍須先以腳前掌著地，隨著重心橫移，全腳著地過渡為支撐腿，併步時兩腳間距為10～20公分（見「雲手」）。

(3) Side Step (Ce Xing Bu)

One leg supports the body. Lift the other leg and move it outward to the side, and place forefoot to the floor first. As the weight shifted, place the entire foot on the floor and the leg becomes the supporting leg. Move the non-supporting foot beside the supporting foot, its forefoot touching the floor first. As the weight is shifted, place the entire foot on the floor and the leg becomes the supporting leg again. The two feet are apart 10–20 cm (See「Cloud Hands」).

4. 擺　步

一腿支撐，另一腿提起，小腿外旋，腳跟先著地，腳尖外擺而後全腳著地（見「轉身搬攔捶」）。

(4) Toes out Step(Bai Bu)

One leg supports the body. Lift the other leg and point the toes outward, and place the forefoot to the floor first. Then place the entire foot on the floor while toes pointing front and outward (see「Turn, Deflect, Parry and Punch」).

5. 跟　步

重心前移，後腳向前跟進半步，腳前掌先著地，隨著重心後移，逐漸全腳著地（見「白鶴亮翅」和「手揮琵琶」）。

(5) Follow Up Step(Gen Bu)

One foot takes a step forward, shifting the weight forward. The other foot follows half a step, and place the forefoot to the floor first. As the weight is shifted, place the entire foot on the floor, and the leg becomes the supporting leg (See「White Crane Spreading Wings」and「Playing the Pipa」).

6. 碾　步

以腳跟為軸，腳尖外撇或內扣，或以腳前掌為軸，腳跟外展（見第一個「左野馬分鬃」及「單鞭」之右腳）。

(6) Pivoting Step(Nian Bu)

Pivot on a heel, moving the toes either inward or outward. One may also pivot on the forefoot, moving the heel either inward or outward (See「Splitting the Wild Horse's Mane – Left」 and the「Single Whip」right foot).

24式太極拳中主要有以上6種步法。

Above are the six main steps in 24-form Taiji Quan.

五、腿　法

蹬腳──支撐腿微屈，另一腿屈膝提起，腳尖上蹺，以腳跟為力點蹬出，腿自然伸直，腳不低於腰部（見「左（右）蹬腳」）。

24式太極拳只出現「蹬腳」一種腿法。

5. Legs

Kicking with the Heels──The supporting leg is bent. Lift the other knee and kick out with the heel. The leg is stretched naturally, the foot higher than the level of the waist (See 「Kicking with the Left /Right Heel」). This is the only leg work form in 24-form Taiji Quan.

六、身型和身法

1. 頭——虛領頂勁，下頜微內收。

2. 肩——保持鬆沉。

3. 肘——自然下墜。

4. 胸——自然舒鬆，微內含。

5. 背——自然放鬆，舒展拔伸。

6. 腰——自然放鬆，不可後弓或前挺，以腰為軸帶動四肢。

7. 脊——保持自然伸直，不可左右歪斜。

8. 臀——臀要下垂收斂，不可後凸；胯不可左右歪斜。

9. 膝——伸屈要柔和自然，膝關節要與腳尖同向。

6. Body

(1) Head—Draw up; chin is slightly tucked in.

(2) Shoulder—Maintain relaxed and leveled.

(3) Elbow—Sunk naturally.

(4) Chest—Maintain naturally, comfortable, depress slightly inward.

(5) Back—Naturally relaxed and stretched.

(6) Waist—Naturally relaxed, do not bend forward or back-

ward, as the pivot point of the body and limbs.

(7) Spine—Maintain upright naturally, do not lean in any direction.

(8) Buttocks—Pulled in; maintain upright hips.

(9) Knee—Extended or bent gently. Keep the knee and toes in the same direction.

七、眼　法

目視前方（前手）或動作的方向，做到精神貫注，意動勢隨，神態自然。

7. Eyes

Eyes look ahead at a hand placed in front or a moving hand. The spirit is focused. The mind and body unite. Facial expression is natural.

第二章

24式太極拳套路動作分解

Chapter 2 24-form Taiji Quan Movements Decomposition

第一節　24式太極拳套路拳譜
Section 1　24-form Taiji Quan Spectrum

　　24式太極拳分為8組，包括「起式」、「收式」共有24個姿勢動作。為方便練習者演練，將24個動作名稱按組分列，習者可按照套路介紹，按「組」分「式」練習。

　　24-form Taiji Quan is divided into 8 groups and 24 movements including 「Opening」 and 「Closing」. To learn more easily, you will find listed here all the groups and names. You can follow the introduction to practice them in groups and movements.

第一組

1. 起　式
2. 左右野馬分鬃
3. 白鶴亮翅

第二組

4. 左右摟膝拗步
5. 手揮琵琶
6. 左右倒捲肱

第八組

21. 轉身搬攔捶
22. 如封似閉
23. 十字手
24. 收　式

Group 1

1. Opening

2. Splitting the Wild Horse's Mane – Left and Right

3. White Crane Spreading Wings

Group 2

4. Brush Knees and Twist Steps – Left and Right

5. Playing the Pipa

6. Backward Steps and Swirling Arms – Left and Right

Group 3

7. Grasp Bird's Tail – Left

8. Grasp Bird's Tail – Right

Group 4

9. Single Whip

第二節　24式太極拳套路動作分解

Section 2　24-form Taiji Quan Detail Explanation Step by Step

預備式

身體自然站立，兩腳併攏，腳尖向前，兩臂垂於身體兩側，手指微屈，中指輕貼於褲縫，頭頸正直，口閉齒叩，舌抵上腭，肩、胯、膝、胸、腹均要自然放鬆，精神集中，兩眼平視，表情自然。

Preparing

Maintain a natural upright position. Place the feet together and toes pointing forward. Arms are beside both sides of the body. Bend the fingers slightly, the middle one on the sewing lines of the pants. Head and neck is upright; the mouth is closed. Tongue is at the roof of mouth. Shoulders, hips, knee, chest, and abdomen have to be naturally relaxed, mind concentrated. Eyes see straight forward. Keep face express naturally.

第 一 組

一、起 式

1. 重心向右腿移動，右腿微屈，左腳跟提起，左腳大拇趾著地，而後左腳輕提起向左側分開，由左腳大拇趾先著地，再依次腳掌、腳跟，全腳著地。雙腳平行站立成開立步，兩腳橫向距離約與肩同寬，兩臂保持自然下垂，眼向前平視（圖2-1）。

Group 1

1. Opening

（1）Shift the weight to the right leg and bend the leg slightly. Raise the left heel first and step to the left, with toes touching the ground first, then the forefoot, then the heel. The entire foot is planted on the ground and stand with legs parallel to form the「opening step」. In this position, the feet are apart at shoulder's width, arms down naturally, eyes looking ahead (Figure 2-1).

2. 兩臂內旋，手背向前，兩臂微向下再向前平舉，與肩同高、同寬，自然伸直，手心向下，指尖向前，眼視前方（圖2-2）。

（2）Push the arms down slightly, then move up to shoulder's

level and the same width, extending naturally. Palms are facing down, fingers pointing forward, eyes looking ahead (Figure 2–2).

3. 上體保持正直，兩腿慢慢屈膝半蹲成馬步。同時，兩掌輕輕下按至腹前，兩肘下垂，與兩膝相對，兩掌掌跟輕輕下按，指尖微微上翹，使掌心略向前下方，眼看前方（圖2-3）。

(3) Maintain a natural upright position in the upper body. Bend legs slowly to a half squat (Ma Bu), pushing palms down gently to the level of the abdomen. The distance between the arms should remain the same. Palms face down and slightly for–

圖2-1 圖2-2 圖2-3

ward, eyes looking ahead (Figure 2–3).

【要領】

（1）左腳開步要點起點落，提腳高度不宜超過右腳踝骨。在左腳未著地前，重心應在右腿上，隨著左腳全腳掌著地，重心逐步由右腿移至兩腳。

（2）兩臂前平舉的同時，尾閭要扣，命門後撐，兩臂與命門有一種對拉的感覺。兩臂前平舉時要鬆肩墜肘。兩腿自然放鬆，不可僵直。

（3）屈膝下蹲應鬆腰，臀部不可凸出，身體重心落於兩腿中間。軀幹保持舒展正直，如坐在書桌前的椅子上，兩掌輕放在書桌上。兩臂下落要與身體下蹲協調一致，同時完成。

Key Points

（1）Lift the left heel first and place the toes down first. The height of the foot being raised should not be over the right ankle's level. The weight remains on the right leg until the left foot is placed down on the ground. Then, it is shifted over between the legs.

（2）While arms are raised, do not push the hip backward. Keep shoulders relaxed, elbows sunken, legs relaxed; do not be stiff.

（3）Bend the knees to a half-squat, keep waist relaxed.

The body should move straight down, do not push out hips. The weight remains centered. The upper body is straight, but not to the point of being uncomfortable. The position is similar to sitting in a chair in front of a desk. Push arms down naturally and bend the legs at the same time.

二、左右野馬分鬃

1. 左野馬分鬃

（1）在腰的驅動下，上體微向左再微向右，並把重心移至右腿上。同時，右臂隨腰的微微轉動向下向左向右畫一小圓弧，並屈臂於胸前；左臂隨腰的旋轉帶動左手微向上向左再向右下走弧至小腹前。左腳同時收至右腳內側。初習者可腳尖點地以穩定重心（圖2-4）。

2. Splitting the Wild Horse's Mane –Left and Right

(1) Splitting the Wild Horse's Mane–Left

a. Led by the waist, slightly turn the upper body first to the left, then to the right. Shift the weight onto the right leg. At the same time, right arm follows, moving first slightly down, then to the left, then to the right. Draw two arcs in opposite directions with the arms. At this point, the arms are in front of the body and the right arm is above the left arm. Meanwhile, bring the left foot and place it beside the right foot. For beginners, tiptoes can touch the ground for stability (Figure 2–4).

（2）上體繼續向右轉動，同時將左臂外旋，使左手心向上，與右手心上下相對，如抱球狀。左腳同時向左前方邁出，腳跟著地，眼看左前方（圖2–5）。

b. Continue to turn the upper body to the right. At the same time, move the left arm outward. The left palm is facing up, the right palm facing down, as if holding a ball. The left foot steps to front left with only the heel touching the ground while watching the front left (Figure 2–5).

（3）上體隨右腳跟後碾向左前湧動並微微轉

圖2–4　　　　圖2–5

腰，下肢成左弓步，左腳尖向前。同時，上體繼續向左轉動，左右兩手隨上體的轉動，分別向左上、右下分開，左手高與眼平，手心向裏斜向上，肘微屈；右手落於右胯旁，肘也微屈，手心向下，指尖向前，眼看左手（圖2-6）。

c. Pivot on the right heel inward and turn the upper body to left front. The lower body forms a bow step, left toes pointing forward. Continue to turn the upper body to the left and separate both hands. Move the left hand to upper left and stop at eye height, palm facing inward and diagonally up. Move the right hand to lower right and stop at the side of the right hip, the elbow bending slightly, the palm facing down, fingers pointing forward. Eyes look at the left hand (Figure 2-6).

2. 右野馬分鬃

（1）上體微向後移至左小腿與地面垂直，左腳尖蹺起，腰帶左腳外撇約45°，隨後，左腳踏實，重心慢慢向左腿移動，使左腿前弓，上體左轉，右腳跟離地，腳尖著地。同時，左臂內旋，帶動左手翻轉，手心向下並屈臂成弧形，右手向前微向左畫弧，眼看前方（圖2-7）。

（2）Splitting the Wild Horse's Mane–Right

a. Move the upper body backward and stop when left leg

forms 90° with the ground, lifting the left toes. Waist leads to move the left foot outward about 45°, then place the entire left foot down to the ground. Shift the weight slowly to the left leg. Left leg bent forward, upper body turned left. Lift the right heel and keep the toes on the ground. At the same time, move the left arm inward, leading the left hand overturned to make the palm facing down, the arm arched. Move the right hand forward slightly then to the left drawing an arc. Eyes look ahead (Figure 2-7).

（2）上體繼續左轉，左臂屈收於胸前，右手向內向左畫弧，右臂輕輕外旋使右手心向裏，指尖向

圖2-6　　　　　圖2-7

下，置於小腹前。同時，上體保持正直，將右腳輕靈地收至左腳內側（初習者腳尖可點地），眼看左手（圖2-8）。

b. Continue to turn the upper body to the left. Bend the left arm in front of the chest. Move the right hand inward to the left drawing an arc. Rotate the right arm gently to the right leading the palm facing inward, fingers pointing downward and stop in front of the lower abdomen. At the same time, maintain upper body upright, and place the right foot gently beside the left foot (Beginners'food can touch the ground). Eyes look at the left hand (Figure 2-8).

（3）上體左轉不停，右腿帶動右腳向右前方邁出，腳跟著地。同時，在腰的帶動下右臂繼續外旋，使右手心向上，與左手心上下相對，成抱球狀，眼看前方（圖2-9）。

c. Continue to turn the upper body to the left. The right leg leads right foot step to front right with only the heel touching the ground. At the same time, the waist leads the right arm to rotate outward and make the palm facing up, corresponding with the left palm, as if holding a ball. Eyes look ahead (Figure 2-9).

（4）上身微右轉向前湧動，左腳蹬，右腿弓，右腳踏實，腳尖向前，成右弓步。上體繼續右轉不停，兩手隨轉體分別向左下右上分開，右手高與眼平，手心向裏斜向上，肘微屈；左手落於左胯旁，肘也微屈，手心向下，指尖向前，眼看右手（圖2-10）。

d. Turn the upper body right slightly then move forward. The left foot pushes the ground, the right leg is arched, planting the right foot on solid ground, toes facing ahead, into a 「bow step」(Gong Bu). Turn the upper body continuously to the right. Move two hands respectively. The right hand stops at level of eyes, palm facing diagonally up, elbow bent. Move the left hand down to the left side of hip. The elbow is bent, palm

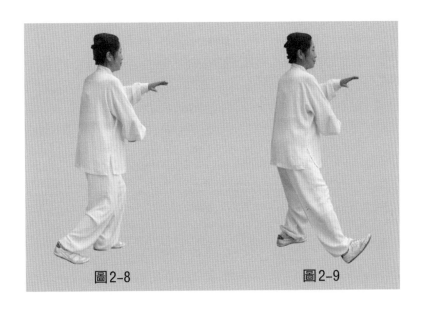

圖2-8　　　　　　　　圖2-9

facing down, and fingers pointing forward. Eyes watch the right hand (Figure 2-10).

3. 左野馬分鬃

與「右野馬分鬃」相同，只是動作左右相反。

(3) Splitting the Wild Horse's Mane-Left

Repeat「Splitting the Wild Horse's Mane-Right」, in the opposite direction.

【要領】

（1）動作轉換時，上體不可前俯後仰，保持胸部寬鬆舒展，兩臂運動要走弧線，不可直來直去。

圖2-10

（2）重心轉換要做到慢、穩、速度勻稱。

（3）收腳、邁腳要輕靈，做到點起點落；提腳不宜過高，也不能擦地。

（4）弓步前腿膝部不可超過腳尖，後腿要鬆靜，自然伸直，不可僵直，腳跟可適當調整，使身體順遂，不彆扭；弓步前後腳應落在中軸線兩側，兩腳橫向距離為20～30公分，要避免踩鋼絲步及麻花步。

（5）兩手相抱時，要注意腋下空開，手距身體20～30公分。

Key Points

（1）Maintain upper body upright; keep the chest relaxed and comfortable. Move arms in an arc; do not move it straight.

（2）Shift weight slowly, steady, with an even speed.

（3）Move feet gently and fast. Always lift the heel or the forefoot of the foot first, and place the palm or heel to the ground first. Neither lift the feet too high nor scratch the floor.

（4）For the bow step, the front leg knee should not go beyond toes. The other leg should be relaxed, extended naturally, not rigidly. Heels can be properly adjusted so that you are physical comfortable. Feet should rest on both sides of the center and stand on two parallel lines separately, which is 20–30 cm apart. Do not put the two feet on the same line, or on the other side of the center.

(5) While holding a ball with both hands, there should be a space between the arms and the body. The distance between the hands and the body is about 20 ～ 30 cm.

三、白鶴亮翅

1. 上體微向左轉，重心略前移，帶動右腳跟離地，並慢慢提起右腳跟進半步，前腳掌著地。同時，左掌在左臂內旋的帶動下，翻掌使手心向下，並屈臂於胸前；右手向前向左畫弧，手心換轉向上與左手上下相抱（圖2-11）。

3. White Crane Spreading Wings

(1) Turn the upper body to the left and shift the weight slightly forward, leading the right heel to rise. Slowly move forward half a step, only the palm of the feet touching the ground. Meanwhile, the left palm is led by the left arm to rotate inward. Turn over the palm to face up. Bend the arm in front of the body; move the right hand to the left, drawing an arc. Turn over the right palm to face up and the left hand to face down as if holding a ball (Figure 2-11).

2. 上體右轉的同時，右腳踏實，重心落於右腿。兩手同時左右分開，眼看右手（圖2-12）。

(2) Turn the upper body to the right and plant the right

foot on the ground solidly. Shift the weight onto the right leg. Meanwhile, separating the two hands, move the left hand to the left, right hand to the right. Eyes watch the right hand (Figure 2-12).

3. 上體向左轉至面向前方，左腳輕輕提起向前移動，腳尖點地，成左虛步。同時，兩手隨轉體慢慢向右上、左下弧線分開，右手提至右額前，手心向左略向後，指尖向上；左手落於左胯外側略前，手心向下，指尖向前，眼看前方（圖2-13）。

(3) Turn the upper body to the left front. Lift the left foot gently and step forward, with only the toes touching the ground

圖2-11　　　　圖2-12　　　　圖2-13

to form an 「empty stance」. At the same time, move the right hand in front of the face, palm facing left and backward slightly, fingers pointing up. Move the left palm slowly backward to the side of the left hip, palm facing down. The fingertips point forward. Eyes watch ahead (Figure 2-13).

【要領】

（1）在全部動作中，上體不可前俯後仰，挺胸凸臀，應保持上體正直。

（2）腰部左右轉動要自然連貫，不要只兩肩擺動。

（3）兩臂運動要旋動，兩手運動走弧線，不可直來直去。

（4）右手上提、左手下按要與上體左右轉動協調一致。

Key Points

（1）For the entire movement, maintain an upright upper body; do not bend forwards or backwards. Maintain stretched and relaxed chest and bent arms.

（2）Turn waist naturally and fluidly. Move the shoulders with the rest of the torso.

（3）Rotate arms. Move hands in arc. Move in a circular fashion.

(4) The raising of the right hand and pushing of the left hand should coordinate with the upper body turning.

第 二 組

四、左右摟膝拗步

1. 左摟膝拗步

（1）上體微左轉，帶動右手經體前向下，經右胯弧線向右後上方舉起，與頭同高，手心向上；左手自左側上擺，經頭前向右畫弧落至右肩前，手心向下。同時，左腳收至右腳內側，頭隨上體轉動，眼看右手（圖2-14）。

圖2-14

Group 2

4. Brush Knees and Twist Steps–Left and Right

(1) Brush Knees and Twist Steps – Left

a. Turn the upper body to left slightly, leading the right hand to push down in front of the body. Then draw an arc to the side of the head, palm facing inward and upward. Move the left arm in front of the head to the right shoulder, palm facing down. At the same time, place the left foot beside the right foot. Eyes watch the right head (Figure 2–14).

（2）重心略下沉，右手收至肩頭，虎口與耳相對，大拇指指向肩井穴；左臂內旋，左手向下略向前弧線下摟。同時，左腳向前偏左邁出，腳跟著地，眼看前方（圖2-15）。

b. Sink the weight downward slightly. Bring the right hand over the right shoulder, with the Tiger's Mouth facing ears and the thumb pointing to the shoulder. Rotate the left arm inward. Move the left hand forward slightly then downward in arc. Meanwhile, move the left foot to the front left, with the heel touching the ground. Eyes watch ahead (Figure 2–15).

（3）上體左轉，左手經腹前過左膝摟過，並回挪停於左胯外側，掌心向下，指尖向前；右手隨重心

前移向前推出，指尖與鼻尖相對，掌心向前，五指向上，臂自然伸直，肘要微屈垂。左腿屈弓，右腿自然蹬直，眼看右手（圖2-16）。

　　c. Turn the upper body to the left. Move the left hand from the abdomen around the left knee to the outside of the left hip, palm facing down, fingers pointing forward. Push the right hand forward and shift the weight forward, fingertips at the nose level, palm facing forward, fingers pointing up. Extend the arm naturally, bending the elbow vertically. Bend the left leg and extend the right leg. Eyes watch the right hand (Figure 2-16).

圖2-15　　　　　　　　圖2-16

2. 右摟膝拗步

（1）重心稍後移，蹺起左腳尖。右掌向前送勁，左臂輕提使左手停於左小腹前。上體微左轉，帶動左腳尖外擺（約45°）。同時，左掌換轉，手心向上，眼看右手（圖2-17）。

(2) Brush Knees and Twist Steps–Right

a. Shift weight backward slightly and lift the left toes. Push the right palm forward. Gently raise the left arm until the left hand is level with the abdomen. Slowly turn the upper body to the left, leading the left toe to point about 45° outwards. Meanwhile, turn over the left palm to face up. Eyes watch the right hand. (Figure 2–17).

圖2-17　　　　　圖2-18

（2）上體繼續左轉，重心前移，左腳踏實，右腳收至左腳內側。右手經頭前畫弧，停於左肩前，掌心向下；左手向左弧線上舉，掌心向上，與頭同高，眼看左手（圖2-18）。

b. Continue to turn the upper body to the left, weight shifting forward. Plant the left foot solidly on the ground and move the right foot beside the left foot. At the same time, push the right hand to the front of left shoulder, palm facing down. Raise the left hand and draw an arc to left, palm facing up at the level of the head. Eyes watch the left hand (Figure 2-18).

（3）與「左摟膝拗步」（2）同，只是左右動作相反。

c. Repeat「Brush Knees and Twist Steps-Left」(2), in the opposite direction.

（4）與「左摟膝拗步」（3）同，只是左右動作相反。

d. Repeat「Brush Knees and Twist Steps-Left」(3), in the opposite direction.

3. 左摟膝拗步
動作說明與右摟膝拗步同，只是左右動作相反。

(3) Brush Knees and Twist Steps–Left

Repeat「Brush Knees and Twist Steps–Right」, in the opposite direction.

【要領】

（1）整個動作過程要以腰帶動四肢，以腰為軸，全身上下協調一致。

（2）弓步時，前腳尖向前，不可外撇、內扣，後腳尖與前腳尖方向夾角為45°，兩腳橫向距離為10～20公分。

（3）上體要始終保持中正，上肢擺動時，身體不可左右晃動，肩要平，頭要正。

（4）摟手和推手打掌要同時完成。

Key Points

（1）The entire movement should be led by waist. The waist is acting as an axle; the whole body moves in coordination with it.

（2）While making a Bow Step (GongBu), the toes of the front foot are pointing forward. The toes of the other foot are pointing at about 45° outwards in relation to the body. Feet are on standing two parallel lines which are about 10 to 20 cm apart.

（3）Keep the upper body upright. When the arms are moving, do not move upper body to the left or right. Shoulders are flat. Head is upright.

(4) One hand brushes and the other hand pushes, both movements finishing at the same time.

五、手揮琵琶

右腳輕輕跟進半步，前腳掌著地，而後重心落於右腿上；上體微向右轉，左腳輕提略向前移，腳跟著地，腳尖蹺起，膝部微屈，成左虛步。同時，左手由左下向前向上挑舉，高與鼻尖平，掌心向右，臂微屈垂，並有外旋之意；右臂屈肘收回右手，置於左臂肘部裏側，掌心向左，有下按前送之意，眼看左手（圖2-19）。

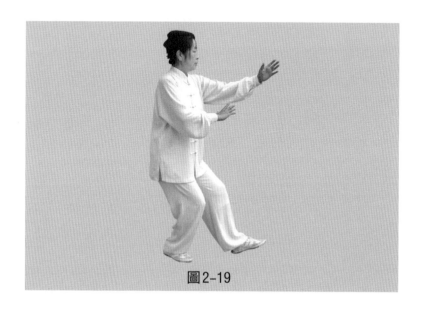

圖2-19

5. Playing the Pipa

The right foot follows up gently in a half-step, placing down on the ground with the palm of the foot first, then the entire foot. Shift the weight onto the right leg. Turn the upper body to the right. Lift the left foot gently and move forward with only the heel touching the ground to form an「Empty Step」. At the same time, raise the left hand from the lower left to the front, and up to the nose-level, palm facing right, arm bent and intending to turn outward. Bend the right elbow and place the hand inside of the left elbow, palm facing the left, ready to push down. Eyes watch the left hand (Figure 2-19).

【要領】

（1）身體要平穩自然，不可上下起伏，要沉肩垂肘，全身放鬆。

（2）左手上挑走下弧，右手四肢走上弧。

（3）定勢時，氣沉丹田，落胯呼氣，腰部略回撑，帶動兩臂內外旋，促使右手向下向前，左手向上向前合勁。

（4）重心移動，步法、手法的完成均應協調一致。

Key Points

(1) Maintain a steady and natural upper body; do not

move up or down. Sink the shoulders and elbows. The body is relaxed.

(2) Move the left hand in a low arc; move the right in a high arc.

(3) In the 「Empty Step」 position, inhale through abdomen, and exhale with the hips relaxed. Twist the waist slightly, leading the arms to rotate inward, the right hand facing lower front, and the left hand facing upper front. Both hands are coordinated.

(4) The weight should shift in coordination with the movement of the foot and the hand.

六、左右倒捲肱

1. 右倒捲肱

（1）上體稍右轉，右手翻掌，手心向上，經腹前由下向後上方畫弧平舉，與頭同高，眼隨右手向後看；左掌翻轉，手心向上，同時，頭回轉向前，眼看左手（圖2-20）。

6. Backward Steps and Swirling Arms—Left and Right

(1) Backward Steps and Swirling Arms – Right

a. Turn the upper body to the right slightly. Turn over the right hand to face up and draws an arc from abdomen upward, stopping behind the body at head level. Eyes follow the right hand and look backward. At the same time, turn over the left hand to face up. Turn the head forward to watch the left hand (Figure 2-20).

（2）右臂捲肱屈肘，將右手收至耳側。同時，左腳輕輕提起收至右腳內側，再向後偏左退一步，腳掌著地（圖2-21）。

b. While swirling the right arm, bend the elbow, and place the hand at the right side of the right ear. At the same time, lift the left foot and place the toes next to the right foot gently. Then, the left foot steps backward with only the palm of the foot on the ground (Figure 2-21).

圖2-20　　　　　圖2-21

（3）上體繼續左轉，重心後移，左腳踏實，右腳以腳掌為軸將右腳擺正，腳跟微離地面，右膝微屈成右虛步。同時，右手推向體前，腕高與肩平，掌心向前，指尖向上；左手向後向下弧線收至左腰側，手心向上，指尖向前，眼看右手（圖2-22）。

c. Continue to turn the upper body to the left and shift the weight backward. Plant the left foot firmly on the ground. Pivot on the palm of the right foot until the toes point forward and lift the heel off the ground slightly, bending the knee into an empty step. At the same time, push the right hand forward until the wrist is at shoulder-level, palm facing forward, fingers pointing up. Move the left hand backward and downward to draw an

圖2-22

arc and place it at the left side of the waist, palm facing upward, fingers pointing forward. Eyes watch the right hand (Figure 2-22).

2. 左倒捲肱

（1）上體稍左轉，左手向左後方畫弧上舉，與頭同高，掌心向上，眼隨左手向側後看；右手翻掌，手心向上，同時頭要回轉，眼看右手（同圖2-20）。

(2) Backward Steps and Swirling Arms – Left

a. Turn the upper body to the left slightly. Move the left hand to draw an arc to the left and a little behind the body, until at head-level, the palm facing up. Eyes follow the left hand and look backward. Turn the right hand over to face up. Turn over the head to look at the right hand (with Figure 2-20).

（2）與「右倒捲肱」（2）同，只是動作相反。

b. Repeat「Backward Steps and Swirling Arms-Right」(2), in the opposite direction.

（3）與「右倒捲肱」（3）同，只是動作相反。

c. Repeat 「Backward Steps and Swirling Arms-Right」(3), in the opposite direction.

3. 右倒捲肱

動作與「左倒捲肱」同，只是動作相反。

(3) Backward Steps and Swirling Arms–Right

Repeat「Backward Steps and Swirling Arms–Right」, in the opposite direction.

4. 左倒捲肱

動作與前「左倒捲肱」同。

(4) Backward Steps and Swirling Arms–Left

Repeat「Backward Steps and Swirling Arms–Left」, in the opposite direction.

【要領】

（1）虛步腳後撤時，不要直接抽退，應拔腳如出泥，要輕微向前撐住，弧線向上向後撤退，後撤步在同側偏外落地，兩腳不可成直線或左右腳相交。

（2）兩臂前後分開時應保持夾角在135°，不可成直線。

（3）兩腳提起、落地要點起點落、輕提輕放，避免「砸夯」步。上體要平行移動，不可前俯後仰，上下起伏，左右轉動擺動幅度不宜過大。

（4）手掌前推、後撤不可夾肋、聳肩，手前推時，要鬆腰胯，呼氣下沉，兩手速度協調，手臂不可

僵直。眼神要先左右，後向前，與兩臂協調配合。

Key Points

（1）While swirling back with the 「Empty Step」, do not make sharp movements, moving the foot as pulling it out of the mud and step lightly forward. Step feet backward in an arc, toes touching the ground at the same side of the body and slightly outward. The feet should not be lined up or intersected.

（2）When the two arms separating at front and back, the angle between the two arms should be about 135°. They should not be at the same line.

（3）Lift the feet quickly and lightly. Do not make heavy steps. Keep upper body upright, while moving; do not bend forward or backward; do not lift and push down the body; do not lean, while turning over.

（4）While pushing the palm forward or stepping backward, do not raise the shoulders; keep hips relaxed; breathe through to abdomen. Move both hands with even speed. Arms should not be rigid. Eyes look at the left or right first, then look forward or backward, coordinating with arms.

第 三 組

七、左攬雀尾

1. 上體微右轉，右手由腰側向後上方畫弧平舉，並屈臂抱於胸前，由臂的旋動，將掌心轉向下；左手弧線下落至小腹前，掌心向裏，指尖向下。同時，將左腳收至右腳內側，眼看前方（圖2-23）。

Group 3

7. Grasp Bird's Tail—Left

（1）Turn the upper body to the right slightly. The right hand draws an arc from the side of the waist to the front of the

圖2-23

chest, turning the palm over to face down. The left hand draws an arc to the lower abdomen, the palm facing inward, finger-tips pointing down. Meanwhile, move the left foot beside the right foot. Eyes look forward (Figure 2–23).

2. 上體繼續右轉，右肘外撐，左臂外旋帶動左手翻轉，手心向上，與右手上下相抱。同時，左腳向前偏左邁出，腳跟著地，眼看右手（圖2-24）。

(2) Continue to turn the upper body to the right. The right elbow push outward. The left arm leads the left hand inward, turning over to face up. The arms should be in a position as if holding a ball, with the right hand facing down. At the same time, the left foot steps to the left front only the heel touching the ground. Eyes watch the right hand (Figure 2–24).

掤——上體左轉，重心前移，左腳踏實，左腿屈膝前弓，右腿自然蹬直，成左弓步。同時，兩手前後分開，左臂半屈向前向上掤出，腕高與肩平，掌心向內；右手向下弧線按於右胯旁略前，掌心向下，五指向前，眼由左前臂向前看（圖2-25）。

Forearm Push (Peng)——Turn the upper body to the left. Shift the weight forward and place the left foot on the ground solidly. The left leg is bent, the right leg straight, forming a left–Bow Step(Gong Bu). At the same time, bend the left arm horizontally in front of the body and push it to the upper front. The left wrist is at shoulder height, palm facing in. The right hand draws an arc downward to the right side of the hip, palm facing down, fingers pointing forward. Eyes look forward over the left forearm (Figure 2–25).

　　将——上體略左轉，左手向左前送出，掌心轉向下；同時，右手經腹前向上向前送至左前臂內側，此時，由腰的向右回轉帶動左臂內旋，右臂外旋，使左手心轉向下，右手心轉向上，兩手斜相對，眼看左手（圖2–26）。

圖2–24　　　　　圖2–25

Pulling with Two Hands（Lü）——Turning the upper body to the left slightly, push the left forearm to the left front, turning the palm to face down. At the same time, move the right hand up from the abdomen, then forward, then to the inside of the left forearm. Turn the waist to the right, and the waist leads the left arm to rotate inward, and the right arm to rotate outward. Simultaneously turn the left palm over to face up and the right palm to face down. Eyes look at the left hand （Figure 2–26）.

上體右轉不停，重心後移，右腿屈膝，左腿自然伸直，使上體後坐。同時，帶動兩手向下經腹前向右

圖2-26

畫弧，右手上舉於身體右側後方，與頭同高；左臂平屈於胸前，掌心向內，眼看右手（圖2-27）。

Continue to turn upper body to the right, shifting the weight backward. The right knee bends, the left leg extends allowing the body to lean backward. At the same time, the right hand is led to draw an arc from front of the abdomen to a position on the right side and slightly behind the body, at head level. The left hand is led to draw an arc from front of the abdomen to the front of the chest, bending the arm, palm facing inward, eyes looking the right hand (Figure 2-27).

擠──上體左轉，正對前方；同時，右臂屈肘，

圖2-27

將右手收在左手內側，右手小指根貼於左手大拇指根，兩手心斜相對，眼看前方（圖2-28）。

Push with Arm and Hand(Ji)——Turn the upper body to the left to face the front, bending the right elbow, and place the right hand to the left wrist. The right little finger is on the root of the left thumb. Eyes look forward (Figure 2-28).

重心前移，左腿屈膝前弓，右腿自然伸直，成左弓步。同時，雙手向前慢慢擠出，與肩同高，兩臂撐圓，肘略低於腕，眼看前方（圖2-29）。

Shifting the weight forward, bend the left knee and extend the right leg to form a left bow step (Gong Bu). At the same

圖2-28　　　　　　　　圖2-29

time, push the both hands outward slowly, at shoulder height, arms rounded. Elbows are little lower than the wrist. Eyes look forward (Figure 2–29).

按——左手翻掌，手心向下；同時，右手經左腕上方向右向前伸出，高與左手平，手心向下，兩手分開，寬略窄於兩肩。然後右腿屈膝，上體慢慢後坐，左腿隨上體後坐自然伸展，左腳尖蹺起。同時，兩臂屈肘，兩手收至胸前，手心斜向前下方，眼看前方（圖2-30）。

Press(An)——Turn the left hand over, so the palm is facing down. At the same time, move the right hand from the left

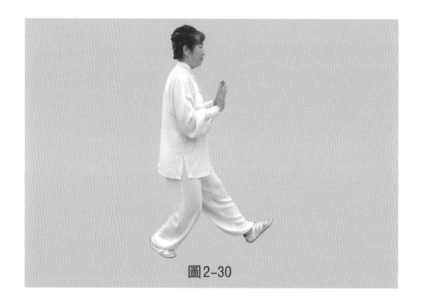

圖2-30

wrist and extend it forward to the height of the left hand, palm facing down. Separate the two hands to shoulder width. Then bend the right knee, push down the upper body backward, extend the left leg, and raise the toes. Simultaneously, bend both arms to the front of the chest, palms facing lower down. Eyes look forward. (Figure 2-30).

上體慢慢前移，兩手向下按至腰腹前，兩手隨右腳前伸，左腿屈膝前弓，向上按出，下肢成左弓步，眼看前方（圖2-31）。

Moving the upper body forward slowly, press both hands down to the front of the abdomen. Then, as the right foot steps

圖2-31

forward, push both hands forward, bending the left leg to form a bow step. Eyes look forward（Figure 2–31）.

【要領】

（1）左臂前掤時，注意用腰帶動左臂，左手像套火爐似的向前向上掤出，臂要撐圓，分手、鬆腰、弓腿三者協調一致，兩腳橫向距離為10～20公分，不宜過寬。

（2）将時，上體不可後仰、右歪，臀部不要凸出；兩臂下将要隨腰轉，走弧線。左腳全腳著地，眼要隨腰轉，回頭看右手。

（3）擠時，上體正直，擠手與鬆腰、弓腿一致；兩手掌要有空隙，不可貼實，兩手前擠與脊背要相對撐。

（4）按時，兩手須走曲線，兩手回收時，上體不可後仰，兩肘下垂，不可外揚，兩手相距3～6公分，兩臂不可僵直，保持一定曲度。

Key Points

（1）During practicing「Forearm Push（Peng）」, pay an attention to use waist leading the left arm and make it rounded. The hands separating, waist relaxing, and bow step making all should be coordinated. Feet are standing on the two parallel lines, which are apart 10–20 cm; should not be wider than that.

(2) While practicing「Pulling with Two Hands (Lü)」, the upper body should not be lean backward or outward. Do not pull buttock out. The two hands follow the waist to move in an arc. The right foot is entirely placed on the ground. Eyes are following the waist; turn head over to look at the right hand.

(3) While practicing 「Push with Arm and Hand」(Ji), keep the upper body upright. The pushing hands, relaxing waist, and bending the leg all are coordinated. Place the right hand on the left one lightly; do not stick on it. As the hands push forward, pull the back backward.

(4) While practicing 「Press」(An), the hands should be moved curvedly. When the hands are pulled back, the upper body should not bend backward. Sink the elbows; do not push them outward. The two hands apart is 3–6 cm. Arms are curved, not rigid.

八、右攬雀尾

1. 上體後坐，並向右轉體，重心向右腿移動。同時，右手向右平行畫弧至右側，左腳尖裏扣135°；右手繼續向下收至腹前，掌心向裏，指尖向下，腋下空開；左臂畫弧，平屈於胸前，手心向下。同時，左腿屈膝，重心移至左腿，並將右腳收至左腳內側，上體

轉正，眼看前方（同圖2-23）。

8. Grasp Bird's Tail – Right

（1）Move the upper body backward and turn to the left. Shift the weight to the right leg. At the same time, the right hand draws an arc to the right side of the body. Pivot inward 135° on the right heel. Continue to move the right hand downward to the front of the abdomen, palm facing inward, fingers pointing down, and armpit open. Move the left arm in an arc, bending in front of the chest, the palm facing down. Bend the left knee, and shift the weight to the left leg. Place the left foot beside the right foot. Turn the upper body to face the front, eyes looking forward（with Figure 2-23）.

2. 與「左攬雀尾」（2）相同，只是左右動作相反。

「掤」、「捋」、「擠」、「按」均與「左攬雀尾」「掤」、「捋」、「擠」、「按」相同，只是左右動作相反。

（2）Repeat「Grasping the Bird's Tail–Left 2」, in the opposite direction.

【要領】

與「左攬雀尾」相同，只是左右相反。

Key Points

Are same as「Grasping the Bird's Tail–Left」, in the oppo-site direction.

第 四 組

九、單　鞭

1. 上體左轉的同時，左腿屈膝，右腿自然伸展，重心移至左腿。隨上體的左轉，左手平行向左畫弧，伸於身體左側，手心向左；右腳也同時裏扣90°，右手向下經腹前運至左肋前，手心向後上方，眼看左手（圖2-32）。

Group　4

9. Single whip

（1）Turn the upper body to the left, bending the left knee and extending the right leg. Shift the weight onto the left leg. The left hand draws an arc across and stops at the left side of the body, palm facing left. Meanwhile, pivot on the right heel inward 90°, moving the right hand downward to stop beside the left ribs, palm facing upper backward. Eyes look at the left hand. (Figure 2–32).

2. 上體右轉，重心徐徐移至右腿，右腿屈膝半蹲，

左腳收至右腳內側。右手向右上方畫弧至右側前，高與肩平，掌心向外；同時，左手向下經腹前向右上畫弧，停於右肩前，手心向裏，眼看右手（圖2-33）。

（2）Turn the upper body to the right, shifting the weight to the right leg, knees half squatting. Place the left foot beside the right foot. The right hand draws an arc to the upper right and stops in front of the right side of the body. The palm is shoulder-level and facing outward. At the same time, the left hand draws an arc downward past the abdomen, then to the upper right, and stops in front of the right shoulder. The palm is facing inward, and eyes are looking at the right hand. (Figure 2-33).

圖2-32　　　　　圖2-33

3. 呼氣沉胯，右手變為勾手，左臂左手掤撐。左腳向左前側方邁出，左腳跟著地，兩手動作與邁左腳同時完成，眼看右手（圖2-34）。

(3) Exhale and sink hip. Turn the right hand into a hook. Push the left forearm and the left hand outward. The left foot steps to front left, only the heel touching the ground. The movement of the hands and the left foot's step finish simultaneously. Eyes watch the right hand (Figure 2-34).

4. 上體左轉，重心左移，左腿屈膝前弓，右腳跟後碾，右腿自然伸直，成左弓步。在重心向左移動的同時，左手隨上體左轉慢慢翻轉向前推出，手心向前，手指與眼齊平，肘微屈垂，眼通過左手看前方（圖2-35）。

(4) Turn the upper body to the left. The left foot takes a step, the left knee bent. Pivot the right foot on its heel, the leg extended to form a bow left step. The weight is shared between both legs. At the same time, the left hand follows the upper body, turns over slowly and pushes forward, palm facing forward. The fingers are at eye-level; the elbow is bent vertically. Eyes watch the front, looking over the left hand (Figure 2-35).

【要領】

（1）完成整個動作要保持上體中正，頂頭、鬆腰、落胯、兩肩鬆沉。

（2）完成動作時，左肘與左膝上下相對，做到肩平、胯正、脊直。

（3）弓步時，左膝尖不可超過左腳尖，後蹬腿要有一定鬆屈度，不可硬挺；右腳跟輾轉要以腰胯合度、舒展為宜，沒有扭勁感覺。

（4）單鞭方向略偏左，弓步時，左腳尖偏左15°。

Key Points

（1）Throughout the sequence of moments, keep the upper

圖2-34　　　　圖2-35

body upright; pull the head upright. Relax the waist, sink the hip, and sink the shoulders.

(2) When the movements are finished, the left elbow and the left knee are on the same vertical line. Keep the shoulders flat, hip upright and spine straight.

(3) For the bow step (Gong Bu), the left knee should not be over the left toes; the right leg should not be rigid, but extended naturally. While pivoting on the right heel, the waist should be comfortable, without the feeling of being twisted.

(4) The single whip movement is directed slightly to the left. For the bow step, the left toes are pointing 15° to the left.

十、雲　手

1. 雲手一

（1）上體右轉，身體重心移至右腿，帶動左腳裏扣。同時，左手向下向右經腹前畫弧至右肩前，手心向裏；右手由勾變掌，手心向外，眼看右手（圖2-36）。

10. Cloud Hands

(1) Cloud Hands 1

a. Turn the upper body to the right, shifting the weight onto the right leg, leading the left toes to swing inward. At the same time, the left hand draws an arc downward, then to the right, cross the front of the abdomen and stop in front of the right shoulder, the palm facing inward. The right hand changes its hook into an open palm to face outward. Eyes look at the right hand（Figure 2–36）.

（2）上體左轉，重心左移，帶動右腳跟離地。同時，左手畫弧運轉到臉前，手心向裏，上體轉至正面；右手向下向左畫弧至小腹前與左手上下相 對（圖2–37）。

b. Turn the upper body to the left, shifting the weight onto the left leg, leading the right foot off the ground. At the same

圖2-36　　　　　圖2-37

time, the left hand draws an arc up to the front of the face, the palm facing inward. Turn the upper body to face the front. The right hand draws an arc downward, to the left, and then stops in the front of the abdomen. The two palms face each other (Figure 2–37).

（3）上體繼續左轉，左手向左畫弧，手掌漸漸外翻，雲至身體左側，掌心向左；右手從下向左上畫弧至左肩前，手心向裏，眼看右手。在上體左轉的同時，重心向左腳移動，右腳向左腳靠近，兩腳相距15～20公分（圖2-38）。

c. Continue to turn the upper body to the left, the left

圖2-38

hand drawing an arc towards the left. Turn over the palm gradually and move to the left side of the body, palm facing the left. The right hand draws an arc to the upper left and stops in front of the shoulder, the palm facing inward. Eyes look at the right hand. As the upper body turns to the left, shift the weight to the left leg. Bring the right foot in, close to the left. The feet should be 15 to 20 cm apart (Figure 2-38).

2. 雲手二

（1）上體右轉，重心向右腿平行移動，帶動右手經臉前向右畫弧至上體右側，上臂先外旋，到臉前時再改為向裏旋，使右手翻轉，手心向右，左手向下向右畫弧至右肩前，眼看右手。同時，重心移至右腿，左腳輕輕提起向左橫跨一步，腳前掌著地（同圖2-36）。

（2）Cloud Hands 2

a. Turn the upper body to the right, and the weight to the right leg, leading the right hand to draw an arc in front of the face. The arc stops at the right side of the body. The right forearm swings outward first, turns over in front of the face, and then swings inward, the palm facing the right. The left hand draws an arc downward first, then to the right, and stops in front of the right shoulder. At the same time, shift the weight to the right leg. Lift the left foot lightly and steps out to the side. Place the palm of the foot to the ground（with Figure 2-36）.

（2）與「雲手一」（2）同。

b. Repeat「Cloud Hands 1」(2), in the opposite direction.

（3）與「雲手一」（3）同。

c. Repeat「Cloud Hands 1」(3), in the opposite direction.

3. 雲手三

（1）與「雲手二」（1）同。

（2）與「雲手一」（2）同。

（3）與「雲手一」（3）同。

(3) Cloud Hands 3

a. Repeat「Cloud Hands 2」(1), in the opposite direction.

b. Repeat「Cloud Hands 1」(2), in the opposite direction.

c. Repeat「Cloud Hands 1」(3), in the opposite direction.

【要領】

（1）上體轉動以腰為軸，腰帶手雲，身手協調一致。

（2）雲手步法是側行步，應點起點落，不可走「砸夯」步；步型上要兩腳平行，不可成「八字步」。

（3）側行步邁左腳時要配合右掌外推按，左掌上提掛；收右腳要配合左掌外推按，右掌上提掛，使左右雲手相反相成。

（4）上體不可左右搖晃，上下起伏，低頭彎腰，上體始終保持正直。

（5）兩眼應隨雲手左右移動。

（6）兩臂腋下要空開。兩手畫圓不可離臉部太近，保持兩臂的曲度掤勁。

Key Points

（1）Waist is acting as an axel when the upper body rotates. Movement of the hands is led by the waist; the body and hands are coordinated.

（2）While stepping sideward, lift or place the foot lightly. There should not be any heavy steps. The feet remain parallel to each other; toes point forwards.

（3）The steps of the feet, the movement of the right hand, and the raising of the left hand are coordinated. The right foot, the left hand, and the right hand are coordinated. The two hands are coordinated and move in opposite directions.

（4）The upper body should not swing or make any unnecessary movements up and down. Do not bow the head. Do not bend the waist. Always maintain an upright upper body.

（5）Eyes follow the pushing hand.

(6) Armpits should be open. The hands should not be too close to the face. Maintain curved and rounded arms with energy.

十一、單　鞭

全部動作說明參看第一個單鞭(2)、(3)、(4)。

11. Single whip

Repeat 9th Single whip (2), (3), (4).

【要領】

與前「單鞭」同。

Key Points

Are same as 9th Single whip.

第　五　組

十二、高探馬

1. 重心前移，右腳跟進半步，身體重心再後移至右腳。右勾手變掌，兩手一起翻轉，手心向上，兩臂同時平舉，兩肘關節微屈，眼看前方（圖2-39）。

Group 5

12. Patting a High Horse

(1) Shift the weight forward. The right foot follows up in a half step. Shift the weight to the right leg. The right hand

changes from a hook into an open palm. Turn over both hands simultaneously to face upward. Raise both arms, elbows bent. Eyes look at the front（Figure 2-39）.

2. 上體微右轉，右臂捲肱，右手經耳旁向前推出，高與頭平，手心向前，指尖向上；同時，上體左轉至正前，左臂屈肘，把左手收至腹前，掌心向上，指尖向右，眼看右手。同時，輕輕提起左腳略向前落地，前腳掌著地成左虛步（圖2-40）。

（2）Turn the upper body to the right and push the right arm from the right ear forward to head level. The palm faces forward, fingers pointing up. Turn the upper body to the front,

圖2-39　　　　　　　　圖2-40

the left elbow bending in front of the abdomen. The palm faces upward, fingers pointing to the right. Eyes watch the right hand. Lift the left foot gently and step forward slightly, touching the ground with only the palm of the foot to form an Empty Step (Figure 2-40).

【要領】

（1）上體保持中正，雙肩向下鬆沉，右肘微屈垂。

（2）跟步時，身體不可起伏。

（3）推右掌、收左手、左腳提落要同時完成；眼神要隨右掌由右側後向前看。

（4）推右掌，手指向上，手心向前；不可手心向下橫掌推出或俯掌推出。

Key Points

（1）The upper body is upright; shoulders are sunken; the right elbow is bent vertically.

（2）While stepping forward, the body should not move up or down.

（3）The push of the right palm, the pull of the left hand, and the raising/placing down of the left foot occur at the same time. Eyes follow the right palm from the back-right side to look at the front.

（4）While pushing the right palm, fingers point upward. The palms face forward, not towards any other direction.

十三、右蹬腳

1. 上體微右轉，將左掌前伸至右手腕上方，兩手背相交叉，隨即上體向左轉，兩手向兩側分開，並向下畫弧，手心斜向下。同時，左腳提起向左前側方落下，腳跟著地（圖2-41）。

13. Kicking with the Right Heel

（1）Turn the upper body to the right slightly. Put the right wrist over the left wrist to form an「X」. Then turn the upper body to the left, separating the two hands to draw arcs down-

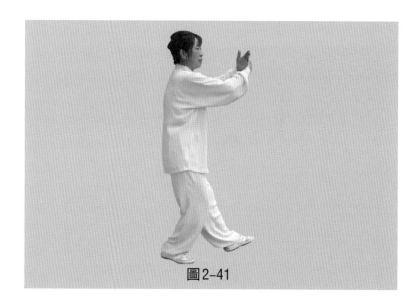

圖2-41

ward. The palms face downward and to the side. At the same time, left foot takes a step towards the left front. Only the heel touches the ground (Figure 2–41).

2. 重心前移，左腳踏實，重心移至左腿，面向左前方。兩手由外向裏畫弧至腹前，兩手交叉，右手在裏，左手在外，手心均向裏，指尖斜向下。同時，右腳收至左腳內側，眼看前方（圖2–42）。

(2) Place the left foot on the ground, shifting the weight forward. Then shift the weight onto the left leg, face looking toward the left front. Move both hands inward to form a「X」in front of the abdomen. The right hand is on the inside, the left hand on the outside, both palms facing the body, fingers pointing diagonally downward. At the same time, place the right foot beside the left foot. Eyes watch the front (Figure 2–42).

3. 兩前臂同時外旋，向上至胸前交叉相抱，成右手在外，左手在裏，手心均向裏，指尖斜向上。同時，左腿獨立支撐，右腿屈膝提起，膝與腰平，眼看右前方（圖2–43）。

(3) Move both forearms outward at the same time to form 「X」in front of the chest. The left hand is on the inside, the right on the outside, both palms facing the body, fingers point-

ing diagonally upward. At the same time, the left leg supports the weight independently. Lift the right leg, raising the knee to waist level. Eyes watch the right front (Figure 2–43).

4. 兩前臂內旋，兩手翻轉，手心向外，分別向左右兩側分開，右手在右前方，左手在左側後方。同時，右小腿伸展，右腳跟用力慢慢蹬出，腳尖回勾，膝關節伸直，與右臂同向並上下相應，蹬腳方向偏右30°，眼看右手（圖2-44）。

（4）Move both forearms inward, turning over the palms to face outward. Move the right hand to the right front, the left hand to left side and slightly behind the body. At the same

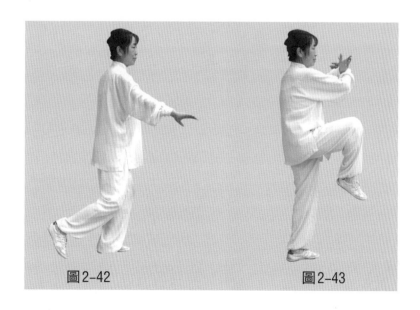

圖2-42　　　　　　　　　圖2-43

time, extend the right leg and kick slowly with the heel, tip-toes pointing back, knee straight, corresponding to the right arm. The kicking direction is 30° to the right. Eyes look at the right hand (Figure 2–44).

【要領】

（1）重心移動要充分，上領下沉，保持重心平穩。上體中正，不可前俯後仰。

（2）兩手分開時手要走弧線，不可直來直去；肘部不可挺直，不要聳肩；右手腕與肩平，左手略高於右手。

（3）支撐腿要微屈，頭部要上領，兩掌要外撐。

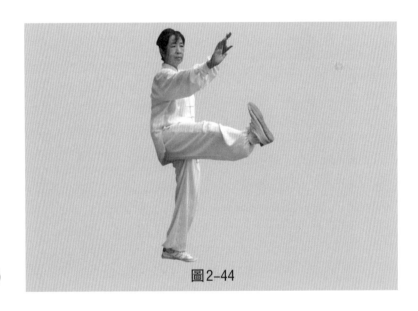

圖2-44

（4）蹬腳方向要偏右30°，不可超過45°，右臂右腿上下相對，兩臂夾角保持135°。

（5）分掌、蹬腳要協調一致，同時完成。

Key Points

（1）Shift the weight completely, and maintain steadiness. Draw the upper body up, and let the lower body sink. Keep the upper body upright; do not bend forward or lean backward.

（2）Always separate hands in an arc; do not make choppy or straight movements. The elbow should not be rigid. Do not raise shoulders. The right wrist is at shoulder level. The left hand is slightly higher than the right hand.

（3）The supporting leg is bent slightly. Draw the head up. Palms are arched outward.

（4）The direction of the kick is about 30° to the right. The right arm corresponds with the right leg. The angle between the two arms is about 135°.

（5）The separating palms and the kick are coordinated and finish at the same time.

十四、雙峰貫耳

1. 右小腿屈膝下垂，腳面自然伸展。左臂向右收至與右臂平行，再下落於右腿兩側，掌心皆翻轉向上，眼看前方（圖2-45）。

14. Striking Ears with Both Fists

（1）Lift the right knee so that the lower leg hangs at 90°, the right foot stretched naturally. Move the left arm to be parallel with the right one. Then move both hands to the sides of the right thigh and turn them over to face upward. Eyes look at the front（Figure 2-45）.

2. 隨左腿屈膝，重心下沉，兩手握拳拉至胯兩側。同時，將右腳向前方上步，腳跟著地，方向仍偏左30°，眼看前方（圖2-46）。

（2）Bend the left knee and bring the weight lower. Form fists with both hands and pull them up beside the hips. At the

圖2-45　　　　　　　圖2-46

same time, the right foot steps forward with only the heel touching the ground, toes pointing 30° to the left. Eyes watch the front（Figure 2–46）.

3. 右腿屈膝，重心前移，右腳踏實。兩臂兩拳從上體兩側向前上畫弧，貫拳於頭前30～40公分，兩拳相距與頭同寬。左腿同時自然伸直，成右弓步，眼平視前方（圖2-47）。

（3）Bend the left knee and shift the weight forward. Plant the right foot on the ground. The fists punch from either side of the upper body to the upper front and stop at 30–40 cm in front of the head. The fists should be one head's width apart. At the

圖2-47

same time, extend the left leg to form a right「Bow Step」(Gong Bu). Eyes look straight ahead (Figure 2–47).

【要領】

（1）定勢方向與右蹬腳方向一致，右腳上步時要隨重心下降輕輕落下，不可「砸夯」步。

（2）兩手平行下落於大腿兩側成拳時，應有下砸之意；兩拳向前上貫拳時，兩臂應內旋運動。

（3）兩手握拳，手心不要過緊，大拇指壓於食指、中指第二指節上。貫拳力點在拳面，拳面呈倒八字形，拳眼斜向下。

（4）定勢時上體不可低頭貓腰，眼要平視；兩臂保持弧形，兩腳橫向距離在10～20公分之間，不宜過寬。

Key Points

（1）The direction of the Bow Step is same as the direction of the kicking. The right foot's step forward should be led by the weight lowering. Place the foot down gently. Do not make heavy steps.

（2）When both fists fall to the sides of the right thigh, intend to punch downward. While punching toward the upper front, move the arms in an intward arc.

（3）Do not hold the fists too tightly. The thumbs press on

the second segment of the index and middle fingers. Deliver the energy to the base segment of the fingers. The two fists form a 「\/」 shape. The eyes of the fists are facing diagonal downward.

(4) When the movement is finished, do not bow the head or bend the upper body. Eyes look straight ahead. The arms are arched. Feet are on the two parallel lines, which are 10–20 cm apart; they should not by any farther apart.

十五、轉身左蹬腳

1. 左腿屈膝，重心後移至左腿。同時，兩臂向左右分。上體左轉180°，帶動右腳裏扣。兩拳慢慢鬆開，平舉於上體兩側，掌心向外，眼看左手（圖2-48）。

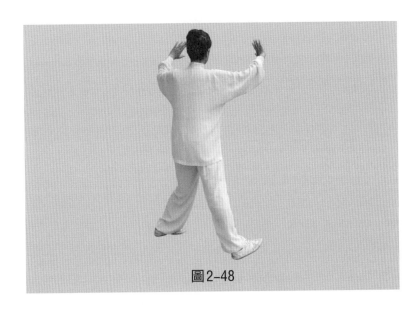

圖2-48

15. Turn and Kick with the Left Heel

（1）Bend the left knee and shift the weight onto his left leg. At the same time, separate the arms apart. Turn the upper body 180° to the left, leading the right foot pivoting on the heel. Turn the fists slowly to opening palms and raise to the both sides of the upper body, palms facing outward. Eyes watch the left hand（Figure 2–48）.

2. 右腿屈膝後坐，重心移至右腳，左腳收至右腳內側。同時，兩手向下畫弧到小腹前交叉合抱，左手在裏，右手在外，手心均向裏，眼看前方（圖2–49）。

（2）Bend the right knees and shift the weight backward to the right foot. Place the left foot beside the right foot. At the same time, move both hands down to the lower abdomen to form「X」. The left hand is on the inside, the right outside. Both palms face the body. Eyes watch the front（Figure 2–49）.

3. 兩臂外旋，變左手在外，右手在裏，手心仍向裏，上提至胸前交叉合抱。右腿屈膝上提，膝與腰平，小腿自然下垂。然後兩臂不停，向左右畫弧分開，置身體兩側，掌心向外，肘關節微屈。同時，左腳慢慢向左前方蹬出，腳跟用力，腳尖回勾，左腳蹬直與左臂上下相應，肘膝相對（圖2–50）。

(3) Move both forearms outward simultaneously to form 「X」 in front of the chest. The left hand is on the outside, the right on the inside, both palms facing the body. Lift the right leg and bend the knee at the waist level. Move the two forearms to the both sides of the body, palms facing outward, elbows bending. At the same time, extend the left leg and kick slowly with the heel, tiptoes pointing backward, knee straight, corresponding to the left arm (Figure 2–50).

【要領】

(1) 轉身時，右腳回扣要充分，上體保持正直，不可低頭彎腰。

圖2-49　　　　　　圖2-50

（2）其餘要點與「右蹬腳」式相同，只是左右相反。蹬腳方向也相反。

Key Points

（1）While turn over the upper body, pivot the right foot fully. Maintain an upright upper body; do not bow or bend.

（2）Other Key Points are same as「Kicking with the Right Heel」in the opposite direction.

第 六 組

十六、左下勢獨立

1. 上體右轉，左小腿屈收於右小腿旁。右手由掌變為勾手，左手經頭上向右弧線下落於右肩前，掌心向右，眼看右手（圖2-51）。

Group 6

16. Push Down and Stand on the Left Foot

（1）Turn the upper body to the right. Bend the left leg and bring it beside the right leg. Change the right hand into a hook. The left hand draws an arc in front of the face and stops in front of the right shoulder, palm facing right. Eyes watch the right hand（Figure 2-51）.

2. 右腿屈膝下蹲，左腳前腳掌落地，沿地面向左

側偏後伸出，腿平鋪伸直，並全腳踏實。左手落於右
肋前，眼看勾手（圖2-52）。

（2）Bend the right leg in a half squat. Place only the palm
of the left foot on the ground and stretch the left leg straight,
and then put the entire foot on the ground. Move the left hand
to the front of the right ribs. Eyes watch the right hand (Figure
2-52).

3. 右腿全蹲成左仆步，上體左轉。右（左）手繼
續向下並外旋使手心向外，指尖向前，沿左腿內側向
前穿出，眼看左手（圖2-53）。

圖2-51　　　　　　圖2-52

（3）Squat with the left leg to for a「Crouch Stance」. Turn the upper body to the left. The left hand continues to move down along the left leg, palm facing inward, fingers pointing forward. Eyes watch the left hand.（Figure 2-53）.

4. 重心前移，左掌繼續前穿。左腳以腳跟為軸腳尖外擺，而後左腿屈膝前弓，重心前移；右腳尖裏扣，右腿自然伸直，成左弓步，眼看前方（圖2-54）。

（4）Shift the weight forward and continue to move the left hand forward. Swing the left toes outwards. Raise the left knee to form a「bow step」. Shift the weight forward. The right toes are pointing inward, the right leg extending naturally. Eyes watch the front（Figure 2-54）.

圖2-53

5. 上體繼續左轉至正前方，左腳尖二次外擺。右勾手內旋於身後，勾尖向上，重心前移，並起身，左掌繼續前穿。右腿屈膝前提，腳尖向下，膝高與腰平；左腿獨立支撐，成獨立步。左手下落按於左胯旁，右勾手變掌向前經體側向上弧線在體前挑起，掌心向左，指尖向上，高與眼平，右臂半屈成弧形，右肘右膝上下相對，眼看右手（圖2-55）。

（5）Continue to turn the upper body to face the front. Swing the left toes outward. Rotate the right hand, still in a hook, behind the body, and point upward. Shift the weight forward and stand up. Continue to move the left hand forward, lifting the right knee to waist level, toes pointing down. The left

圖2-54　　　　　圖2-55

leg supports the body independently to form an 「Independent Step」. The left hand falls slowly to the side the left hip. Change the right hand into an opening palm, moving in an arc upward in front of the body, palm facing left, fingers pointing upward at eye level. The right arm is arched, the elbow above the right knee. Eyes watch the right hand (Figure 2-55).

【要領】

（1）右手由掌變勾手時，勾手方向大約在體側後45°。

（2）右腿全蹲時，右膝尖與右腳尖同向，上體不可前傾；左腿平鋪伸直，腳尖須向裏扣；兩腳掌均須踏實，右腳跟和左腳外側不得掀起，左腳尖與右腳跟緊靠中軸線兩側。

（3）獨立支撐左腿膝部要微屈，不可硬挺；右腿提起時，腳尖自然下垂，不要繃緊腳面；上身正直，頭向上領；右手指尖與鼻尖相對。

Key Points

（1）When changing the left palm into a hook, the fingers points about 45° to the left front.

（2）When the right leg squats, the knee and toes are pointing the same direction. The upper body should not lean forward. Stretch the left leg, the toes pointing 45° inward. The palms of both feet are planted on the ground solidly. The right heel and outside of the left foot should not be lifted off the ground. The left toes and right heel are on the same line.

（3）The supporting leg should be bent slightly without stiffness. When raising the right leg, the toes point downward. The foot should remain natural. Keep the upper body upright. Draw the head up. The fingers of the right hand are at the nose level.

十七、右下勢獨立

1. 右腳下落於左腳內側約一腳處，腳前掌著地；上體左轉的同時，左腳以腳掌為軸，腳跟回擺（圖 2-56）。

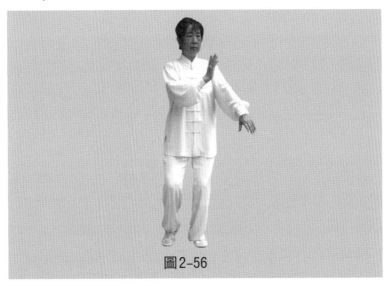

圖2-56

17. Push Down and Stand on the Right Foot

（1）Place the right foot slowly beside the left one with a foot apart, only the palm of the right foot touching the ground. While turning the upper body, pivot on the palm of the left foot and swing the heel outward（Figure 2–56）.

2. 左腿屈膝半蹲，右腳輕輕提起於左小腿內側。同時，左掌微微上提變為勾手，勾尖向下，右手下落於左肩前，眼看勾手（圖2-57）。

（2）Bend the left knee in a half squat. Lift the right foot gently to the inside of the left lower leg. At the same time, raise the left palm slightly and change it into a hook. The hook

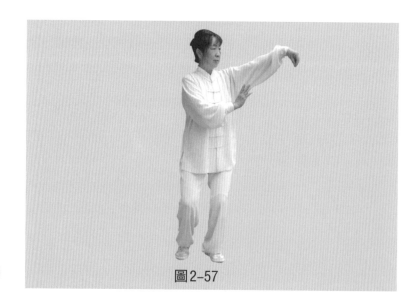

圖2-57

is pointing downward. The right hand falls in front of the left shoulder. Eyes look at the hook（Figure 2–57）.

3、4、5與「左下勢獨立」3、4、5同，只是左右動作相反。

Repeat「Push Down and Stand on Left Foot」3, 4, 5, in opposite directions.

【要領】

（1）左腿屈膝半蹲、右腳輕提起、左掌變為勾手和右手落於左肩前這四個動作要同時完成，協調一致。

（2）其餘要點與「左下勢獨立」同，只是左右相反。

Key Points

（1）The squatting the left knee, lifting the right foot, turning the left hand into a hook and pushing right hand down are finished at the same time and coordinated.

（2）Rest of the Key Points is same as「Push Down and Stand on left Foot」, in the opposite direction.

第 七 組

十八、左右穿梭

1. 右穿梭

（1）上體左轉，左腳向前方落下，腳跟著地，腳尖向左前方，重心前移，左腳慢慢踏實，重心落於左腿，右腳收至左腳踝骨內側。同時，左手翻轉，手心向下，右手向前向左畫弧並收於襠前，掌心向裏，指尖向下；左前臂內旋，左手下按，手心向下，左臂弧形屈按於胸前，眼看前方（圖2-58）。

Group 7

18. Working with a Shuttle–Left and Right

（1）Working with a Shuttle–Right

a. Turn the upper body to the left. The left foot steps forward with only the heel touching the ground. Toes point forward. Shift the weight forward and slowly place the entire left foot on the ground. Bring the right foot beside the left ankle. At the same time, turn the left hand over to face downward. The right hand draws an arc to the front left and stops between the thighs, the palm facing the body, fingers pointing down. Turn the left forearm inward, and push the left hand downward, palm facing down. The left arm is arched in the front of the chest. Eyes watch the front（Figure 2-58）.

（2）上體繼續微左轉，左腿屈膝半蹲，右腳向右前方邁出，腳跟著地。同時，右臂外旋，手心翻轉向上，與左手上下相對如抱球狀，眼看右前方（圖2-59）。

b. Turn the upper body to the left slightly. Bend the left leg in a half squat. The right foot steps forward with only the heel touching the ground. At the same time, move the right arm outward and turn the palm over to coordinate with the left hand, as if holding a ball. Eyes watch the right front（Figure 2-59）.

圖2-58　　　　　圖2-59

（3）上體右轉，重心向右腿移動，右腳踏實，右腿屈膝前弓，左腿自然伸直，成右弓步。同時，右臂向前向上畫弧，將右手翻轉上舉，架於頭右額角前上方，手心向外斜朝上；左手向下經頭前弧線向右前方推出，高與肩平，手心向外，眼看左手（圖2-60）。

c. Turn the upper body to the right. Shift the weight to the right leg. Plant the right foot on the ground. Bend the right knee and extend the left leg to form a Bow Step. At the same time, the right arm draws an arc to the upper front, turning over the hand. Stop at the upper front of the head, palm facing diagonally upward. The left hand draws an arc downward, in front of the head, and pushes to the front right at shoulder level, palm facing outward. Eyes watch the left hand (Figure 2–60).

2. 左穿梭

（1）重心稍後移，右腳尖蹺起，然後上體略向左轉再向右轉，右腳尖有外擺之意，無明顯外擺之實，全腳踏實，重心前移落於右腿，左腳收至右腳踝骨內側。同時，右手下落於胸前，右臂環屈，手心向下；左手向下畫弧落於腹前，手心向裏，指尖向下（圖2-61）。

(2) Working with a Shuttle–Left

a. Shift the weight backward. Lift the right toes and turn

the upper body to the left slightly, then to the right. Intend to turn the right toes, but take no obvious action. Place the entire foot on the ground, shifting the weight onto the right leg. Bring the left foot beside the right ankle. At the same time, the right hand moves to the front of the chest; arm is rounded, palm facing down. Move the left hand down in front of the abdomen, palm facing the body, fingers pointing down（Figure 2–61）.

（2）和（3）與「右穿梭」（2）和（3）動作相同，只是左右動作相反。

Repeat the「Working with a Shuttle–Right」（2）and（3）, in the opposite directions.

圖2-60　　　　　　圖2-61

【要領】

（1）完成整個動作全過程，上體要正直，不可左右歪斜、前傾彎腰、凸臀，上下肢與上體要協調一致。

（2）弓步推掌方向分別在中軸線左右30°～40°之間，架掌之臂要撐圓，肩部不可聳起。

（3）弓步時，前腿膝部不可超過腳尖，重心主要落於前腿，兩腳橫向距離約20公分，不宜過窄或過寬。

Key Points

（1）During the entire movement, keep the upper body upright; do not bend forward. Pull buttocks in. The limbs are coordinated with the upper body.

（2）When pushing the hand out, the direction is about 30°～40° from the centre of the body. The blocking arm should be arched. Do not raise the shoulder.

（3）Same as Bow Step（Gong Bu）.

十九、海底針

1. 重心前移，上體右轉至正前方，右腳跟進半步，前腳掌著地，隨之重心後移，右腳踏實，右腿屈膝，重心落於右腿，左腳成虛步。上體繼續向右轉，右手下落並弧線收至右胯側，手心向左；左手下按於胸前40公

分處，掌心向下，指尖向右，眼看左手（圖2-62）。

19. Needle to the Bottom of the Sea

（1）Shift the weight forward and turn the upper body to face the front. The right foot follows up half a step with only palm of the foot touching the ground. Then shift the weight backward. Place the right foot on the ground solidly, bending the right knee. The weight is on the right leg. The left foot is an empty step. Continue to turn the upper body to the right. The right hand draws an arc downward to the outside of the right hip, palm facing the left. The left hand presses downward to 40cm in front of the chest. The palm is facing downward, fingers pointing right. Eyes watch the left hand（Figure 2-62）.

圖2-62

2. 上體右轉不停，右手弧線上提於右耳側，左手下按於腹前；而後上體左轉，左手向前向左畫弧過左膝，落於左胯側，掌心向下，指尖向前；同時，右手向前向下插掌，掌心向左，指尖向前下方，上體同時也前傾30°～40°。插掌的同時，左腳輕輕提起，略向前落下，眼看前下方（圖2-63）。

（2）Continue turning the upper body to the right. The right hand draws an arc upward to the side of the right ear. Press the left hand downward to the front of the abdomen. Then turn the upper body to the left. The left hand draws an arc outward to the outside of the left hip, palm facing down, fingers pointing forward. At the same time, the right hand thrusts down

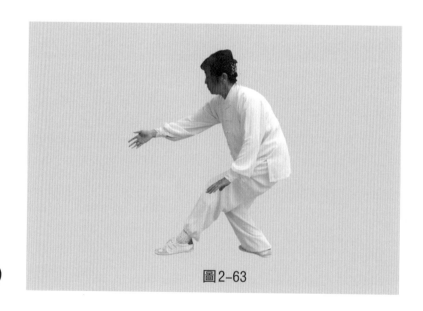

圖2-63

toward the lower front, palm facing left, fingers pointing down-ward. The upper body leans forward 30° to 40° . Meanwhile, lift the left foot gently and take a slight step forward. Eyes look at the lower front（Figure 2–63）.

【要領】

（1）海底針定勢時，上體要舒展、伸拔，前傾不可超過45°，不可駝背、聳肩縮脖、低頭下看。

（2）上體左轉、右手畫立圓向下插掌、左手過膝掤按與左腳輕提下落要協調一致，同時完成。

（3）右手插掌時要意在指尖，指尖領插，右肩放鬆向前下送勁，眼看前下方。

Key Points

（1）When the movement is settled, the upper body is stretched and drawn up. The upper body leans forward no more than 45°. Do not arch the back. Do not raise the shoulders. Do not bow the head.

（2）The upper body turning to the left, the right hand drawing the circle, the left hand pushing and the left foot rising or placing down are all coordinated and finish at the same time.

（3）When the right hand thrusts down, it should be led by the fingers. Focus on the fingertips. Relax the right shoulder and push forward to deliver the energy to the fingertips. Eyes look at the lower front.

二十、閃通臂

1. 上體稍右轉，將上體恢復正直，重心落於右腿，左腳收至右腳內側。同時，右臂提起至胸前，手心向左，指尖向前；左臂屈收，左手舉於右前臂內側，手心向右，指尖向上，眼看前方（圖2-64）。

20. Flashing the Arm

（1）Straighten the upper body and turn to the right slightly. Shift the weight onto the right leg. Bring the left foot beside the right one. At the same time, raise the right arm in front of the chest, palm facing the left, fingers pointing forward. Bend the left arm; put the left hand on the inside of the right forearm, palm facing the right, fingers pointing upward. Eyes look at the front (Figure 2-64).

2. 上體略右轉，重心稍下沉，左腳向前上步，腳跟著地，重心前移，左腿屈膝，左腳踏實，右腿自然伸展，成左弓步。同時，右手向內翻轉，手心向右，右臂環屈撐於頭右側上方；左手向前推出，掌心向前，指尖向上，兩手對拉，眼看左手（圖2-65）。

（2）Turn the upper body to the right and lower the weight slightly. The left foot steps forward with only the heel touching the ground. Shift the weight forward, bend the left knee, and extend the right leg to form a「Bow Step」. At the same time, turn the right hand inward, palm facing the right, arm arched above the right side of the head. Push the left hand forward, palm facing forward, fingers pointing upward. Eyes watch the left hand (Figure 2–65).

【要領】

（1）閃通臂完成時，左肘左膝上下相對，左臂不可挺直，肘部要鬆垂，左肩要沉鬆。

（2）右手上撐時，不要離右額過近，右肘尖向後拉引，與左掌前推按形成對拉勁。

圖2-64　　　　　　　　　　圖2-65

（3）上體保持正直，不可前傾，胯部不可過分扭轉側身，保持重心平穩，上下順遂。

（4）弓步時，左膝與左腳尖齊，不可過；右腿既不鬆軟又不僵直，兩腳橫向距離20公分。推掌、舉掌、弓步要協調一致，同時完成。

Key Points

（1）When the movement is completed, the left elbow is right above the left knee. The left arm should not be straight. The elbow is relaxed; the left shoulder is sunken.

（2）When the right hand is above the right of the head, it cannot be too close to the forehead. The right elbow points towards the back, in correspondence with the left hand.

（3）Maintain an upright upper body; do not lean forward. Hip should not twist in any way. Keep a stable centre of gravity. Keep the whole body comfortable.

（4）Same as「Bow Step」.

第 八 組

二十一、轉身搬攔捶

1. 重心後移，右腿屈坐，上體右轉帶動左腳尖裏扣135°。兩手同時向左側擺動，右手擺至上體右側，左手擺至頭左側，手心均向外，眼看右手（圖2-66）。

Group 8

21. Turn, Deflect, Parry and Punch

(1) Shift the weight backward and bend the right leg. Turn the upper body to the right, leading the left toes to turn inward 135°. Move both hands to the left; the right one stops at the right side of the upper body; the left one stops at the left side of the head. Both palms are facing outward. Eyes watch the right hand (Figure 2-66).

2. 重心左移，左腿屈坐，右腿自然伸直，右腳跟隨之擺順，然後將右腳收至左腳內側。同時，右手握拳向下畫弧落於腹前，小臂內旋，使拳心向外；左手

圖2-66

撐舉於左額前上方，手心向外，指尖向行拳前方（圖 2-67）。

（2）Shift the weight to the left and bend the left leg. Extend the right leg naturally and the right heel follows up, toes facing the front. Then bring the right foot beside the left foot. At the same time, form the right hand into a fist and draw an arc downward to the front of the abdomen. Rotate the right arm inward, the centre of the fist facing outward. The left hand is arched at the upper front left side of the head, palm facing outward, fingers pointing toward the right fist (Figure 2-67).

3. 上動不停，上體右轉，右腳向前邁出，腳跟著地。右拳向上經胸前左側與下落的左掌交叉，左手在外，右拳在裏；右拳不停繼續向上向前搬出，拳面朝前下，右臂沉肩墜肘；左手向下弧線收至左腰側，掌心向前下，指尖向前上，眼看右拳（圖2-68）。

（3）Continue to turn the upper body to the right. The right foot steps forward with only the heel touching the ground. Move the right fist upward past the left side of the chest to make an 「X」 with the left palm. The left palm is on the outside; the right fist is on the inside. Rotate the right fist upward, forward and then strike downward with the back of the hand facing down. Sink the shoulder and elbow. The left hand moves downward to the left side of the waist, palm facing lower front, fingers pointing to the upper front. Eyes look at the right hand (Figure 2–68).

4. 上體繼續轉動至偏右，重心前移，右腳尖外擺並踏實，左腳經右腳內側向前上步，腳跟著地。同時，右臂內旋，右拳向右向後畫弧，挎於右腰側，拳心向上；左臂內旋向後，再向前攔掌於胸前約40公分處，手心向下，指尖向前，眼看左手（圖2-69）。

(4) Continue to turn the upper body to the right. Shift the weight forward. Swing the right toes outward and put the entire foot on the ground solidly. The left foot pauses at the right foot

圖2-67　　　圖2-68　　　圖2-69

and steps forward with only the heel touching the ground. At the same time, rotate the right arm inward. The right fist draws an arc to the left then backward to stop at the right side of the waist. The centre of the fist is facing up. Rotate the left arm inward, backward and then forward and stop in front of the body, about 40 cm away. The palm faces downward, fingers point forward. Eyes watch the left hand (Figure 2-69).

5. 上體左轉正，重心前移，左腳踏實，左腿屈膝前弓，右腿自然伸直，成左弓步。同時，右拳翻轉，向前衝出，拳面向前，拳眼向上；左手坐腕立掌，手心向右，指尖向上，在右小臂內側，眼看前方（圖2-70）。

（5）Turn the upper body to face the front. Shift the weight forward. Place the left foot on the ground solidly. Bend the left knee; extend the right leg to form a left「Bow Step」. At the same time, turn over the right fist to make the eye of the fist face upward and punch forward. The left palm is inside of the right arm and is facing the right, fingers pointing upward. Eyes look at the front (Figure 2-70).

【要領】

（1）虛實轉換要平穩，上體不要上下起伏；上

下肢運動要與上體左右轉動協調一致。

（2）右拳挎腰，左掌前攔，兩臂內旋要以腰帶動；兩肘尖平穩撐沉，兩肩不可聳，上體勿左右搖晃。

（3）收腳，邁步，兩腳要輕靈，重心移動要平穩。

（4）弓步時，兩腳橫向距離要恰當；沖拳要打在身體前方正中，不可順右肩衝出。

Key Points

（1）While the weight is shifted from leg to leg, the upper body should not be moving up or down. The limbs' movement should coordinate with the upper body's turning.

圖2-70

（2）When moving the right fist to the waist or the left palm forward, both arms should be led by the waist. The elbows are slightly bent and are sunken. Do not raise the shoulders and do not shift the upper body to the left or right.

（3）When moving a foot, lift it lightly. The weight should be shifted smoothly and steadily.

（4）When practicing「Bow Step」(Gong Bu)，the distance of the feet should be suitable. Punch to the front of the center of the body；do not follow the right shoulder.

二十二、如封似閉

1. 左手翻轉，掌心向上，經右前臂下向前穿出；右拳變掌，翻轉手心向上，經左前臂回收於胸前。同時，上體右轉，重心後移，右腿屈坐，左腿自然伸直，腳尖翹起，眼看左手（圖2-71）。

22. Withdraw and Push

（1）Turn over the left hand to face up, and thrust it forward under the right forearm. Change the right fist to an open palm and turn it over to face upward, passing the left forearm to the front of the chest. At the same time, turn the upper body to the right, shifting the weight backward. Bend the right leg and extend the left leg, lifting the toes. Eyes watch the left hand (Figure 2-71).

2. 上體向左回轉，兩掌內翻置於胸前，掌心均向下。然後右腳蹬，左腿屈膝前弓，左腳踏實成左弓步。同時，兩掌下按至小腹前繼續向前上推按，兩臂自然伸直，高與肩平，寬略窄於兩肩，掌心向前，指尖向上。同時，重心落於左腿，眼看前方（圖2-72）。

（2）Turn the upper body to the left. Turn both hands over and put them in front of the chest, palms facing downward. Then right foot pushes the ground. The left knee is bent, the left foot placed on the ground solidly to form a 「Bow Step」. At the same time, press both hands downward in front of the lower abdomen, then push to the upper front. Extend the arms naturally at shoulder-height and little less than shoulders' width.

圖2-71　　　　　圖2-72

The palm is facing forward, fingers pointing upward. Shift the weight to the left leg. Eyes look at the front（Figure 2–72）.

【要領】

（1）身體後坐，上體不可後仰，兩掌前按，上體不可前傾。

（2）重心後移，兩臂交叉分拉時，要斜身調臂，鬆肩墜肘落胯，不可聳肩、掀肘或夾肘。

（3）兩掌推按時，要沿弧線用腰勁推按，兩手不要過窄、過寬，更不可合掌。

Key Points

（1）When shifting the body backward, the upper body should not lean backward. When both hands push forward, the upper body should not bow forward.

（2）When shifting the weight backward and separating the arms, the upper body should lean backward slightly to adjust the arms. Relax the shoulders; do not raise them. Sink the elbows and hips; do not raise or fold the elbows.

（3）Push the hands in an arc, led by the waist. The distance between the two hands is not too narrow or too broad. Do not put both hands together.

二十三、十字手

1.重心後移的同時，上體右轉，右腿屈坐，左腳內扣。右手向右畫弧擺至頭前，眼看右手（圖2-73）。

23. Crossing Hands

（1）Shift the weight backward and turn the upper body to the right. Bend the right leg in a half squat, toes pointing inward 45°. The right hand draws an arc to the right, and stops in front of the head. Eyes look at the right hand (Figure 2-73).

2.上體右轉不停，右腳尖外擺，右腿屈膝側弓，

圖2-73

左腿自然伸直，成右側弓步。右手繼續向右側畫弧至身體右側，兩臂成平舉，手心均向外，頭隨右手轉向右，眼看右手（圖2-74）。

（2）Continue to turn the upper body to the right. Swing the right toes outward, bending the knee and extend the left leg to form a right Bow Step（Gong Bu）. The right hand continues to draw an arc to the right side of the body until it is at shoulder level, palm facing outward. Head follows the right hand, turning to the right; eyes watch the right hand（Figure 2-74）.

3. 上體向左回轉，重心移至左腿，左腿屈膝側弓，右腿自然伸直並裏扣右腳。兩手向下同時畫弧，

圖2-74

相合經胸前交叉上舉，成斜十字相交，右手在外，手心均向裏，眼平視前方（圖2-75）。

（3）Turn the upper body back to the left and shift the weight onto the left leg. Bend the left knee. Extend the right leg, toes pointing slightly inward. Both hands draw arcs downward simultaneously and meet in front of the chest to form an 「X」. The right hand is on the outside. Both palms face the body. Eyes look straight ahead. (Figure 2-75).

4. 上體繼續轉向起勢方向，重心移至左腿，右腳提起向左腳收攏半步，前腳掌落地，慢慢全腳踏實，然後兩腿緩緩直立，重心置於兩腳，兩腳平行，腳尖

圖2-75

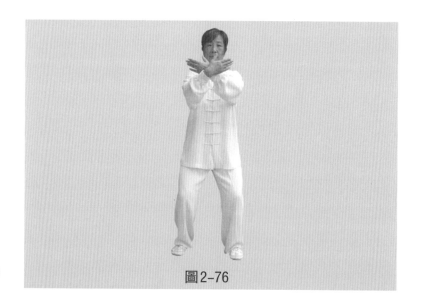

向前，與肩同寬。同時，兩交叉手向上抱於胸前，兩臂撐圓，保持兩腕交叉的斜十字形，眼看前方（圖2-76）。

（4）Turn the upper body back to the direction of the 「Opening」 form and shift the weight onto the left leg. Bring the right foot a half step towards the left foot with only the palm of the foot touching the ground first. Then place the entire foot on the ground. Stand up slowly, the weight shared by both feet. The feet are parallel to each other, toes pointing to the front, shoulder width apart. At the same time, the two arms, crossed, move in front of the chest; the arms are arched. Eyes watch the front (Figure 2-76).

圖2-76

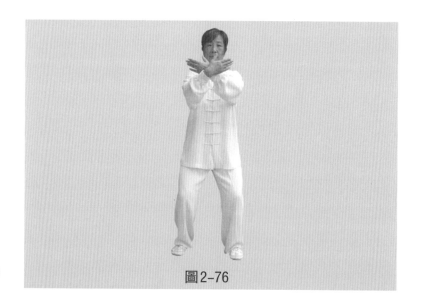

【要領】

（1）轉體、扣腳、弓腿、分手、合手要連貫銜接，不可有停頓。

（2）兩手從身體兩側畫弧下落時，不可貓腰低頭；收右腳時保持上體正直，不可左右傾斜。

（3）兩手在胸前相抱，要圓背、撐肘，放鬆肩部，高與肩平，手腕離胸20公分。

（4）左右兩腳回扣時要合度，保證兩腳平行，腳尖向正前。

Key Points

（1）The movement of the turning body, swinging foot, bending legs, and moving hands is connected smoothly without pause.

（2）When the two hands draw arcs from both sides the body, the upper body should not bow. When bringing the right foot to the left foot, maintain an upright upper body; do not move to the left or right.

（3）When the two hands cross in front of the chest, both arms have to be arched; elbows rounded; shoulders relaxed; the wrists 20 cm from the chest.

（4）Move the feet to be parallel, shoulder width apart, toes pointing forward.

二十四、收　式

1. 兩手交叉緩緩向前掤出，兩臂內旋，兩手翻轉分開，手心向下平舉於身前，與肩同高同寬，眼看前方（圖2-77）。

24. Closing

（1）The crossed-arms push slowly forward and rotate inward. Turn over both hands to face downward and separate them in front of the body, at shoulders' width and height. Eyes watch the front（Figure 2-77）.

2. 兩臂徐徐下落至大腿外側，成起式前狀，左腳輕輕收回，與右腳併攏，與預備式相同（圖2-78）。

（2）Drop the arms slowly to the sides of the body, similar to the opening form. Bring the left foot gently back next to the right foot. This is the same as the「Preparing」position（Figure 2-78）.

【要領】

（1）兩掌由交叉再分開時，兩臂內旋應順勢向前撐；翻轉兩手時，手腕不可屈折，手指不要上翹。

（2）兩臂下落時要沉肩、墜肘，臂微屈，帶動兩手回落，不可僵直下按。

（3）收式要鬆靜、沉穩，保持行拳時的均勻速度。

（4）完成全套動作後要略停片刻，不要匆忙走動。

Key Points

（1）When the two hands are separating from the「X」, both arms should be arched and push forward. When turning over the hands, do not bend the wrists; do not bend fingers up-wards.

（2）When the arms fall down, sink the shoulders and el-bows. Bend the arms slightly to lead the hands down to the sides of the body. Do not be stiff.

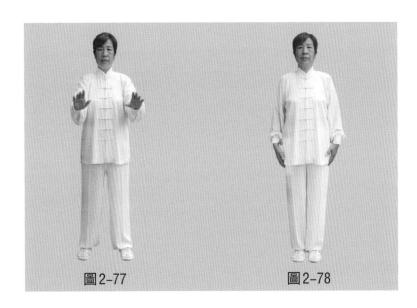

圖2-77　　　　圖2-78

(3) Keep calm, and move with the same speed as other movements.

(4) After completing the full form, keep quiet for a moment. Do not rush to walk.

附1 太極拳的服裝與禮儀

Appendix 1　The Dress and Etiquette in Taiji Quan

一、太極拳的服裝款式及規格要求

1. 料、色可根據個人喜好自選。

2. 上衣為長袖、中式對襟，七對中式直扣絆，周身加邊為3分，前襟後襟可繡（印）文字或圖案。

3. 上衣長袖為燈籠袖，袖口加中式直扣絆。

4. 褲為中式，橫、立褶適宜，褲口褲腰可用鬆緊帶。

5. 上衣長度不宜超過本人直臂下垂的小指指端。

6. 鞋為軟底布、膠或軟皮面練功鞋。

1. Recommendation for dress style and size

One can choose the material and color in personal favor

The upper dress should be long-sleeved and buttoned down the centre with seven pairs of Chinese fasteners. It should be loose and comfortable. The front and back may or may not be printed or embroidered with characters and/or patterns.

The sleeves should be loose, and Chinese fasteners are used in cuffs.

The trousers should be loose and in the Chinese style. A

rubber band can be used in the waist and on the bottom part of the trouser legs.

The upper dress should not hang past the tip of the little finger.

The shoes should be soft, suitable for exercise.

二、太極拳的禮儀

1. 抱拳禮

此禮法是由中國傳統「作揖禮」和少林拳禮加以提煉、規範、統一得來，並賦予了新的含義，為國內外一致採用的具有代表性的禮法。

行禮方法：併步站立，左手四指併攏伸直成掌，拇指屈攏；右手成拳，左掌心掩貼右拳面，左指尖與上頜平齊，右拳眼斜對胸窩，置於胸前屈臂成圓，肘尖略下垂，拳掌與胸相距20～30公分，頭正，身直，目視受禮者，面容舉止大方（附圖）。

抱拳禮的具體含義：

（1）左掌四指表示德、智、體、美四育齊備，象徵高尚情操；拇指屈曲表示不自大，不驕傲，不以「老大」自居。右拳表示勇猛習武，左掌掩右拳相抱，表示「勇不滋亂」、「武不犯禁」，以此來約束、節制自身。

（2）左掌右拳攏屈，兩臂屈圓，表示「五湖入

海」，天下武林是一家，謙虛團結，以武會友。

（3）左掌為文，右掌為武，文武兼學，虛心，
渴望求知，恭候師友、前輩指教。

2. the etiquette for Taiji Quan

（1）「Baoquanli」(hands held together in greeting)：this
was developed by combining the traditional greeting of Zuoyi
and Shaolin. It has become a practice recognized internationally.

Method：Stand with the feet close together. Make a fist
with the right hand and touch the left palm. Position hands
20–30cm in front of the chest. The two arms should be slightly
bent, elbows sinking slightly. Keep the head and the body upright. Look at the receiver confidently and respectfully.

The meaning:

a. The four fingers represent morality, intelligence, fitness,

附圖

and aesthetics, symbolizing the loftiness of the spirit. The bending thumb shows modesty. The right fist represents the hard work in practicing Wushu, and the clasping hands represent holding oneself with courage and not abusing one's strength.

b. The left palm holding the right fist closely while the two arms are slightly bent represents that all people practicing Wushu are in the same family, as all currents flow into the sea. Therefore, they should unite together and make friends by exchanging skills.

c. The left palm symbolizes the civil component of education while the right fist represents the military component. Together, it means having an open mind and the eagerness to be instructed by masters, teachers and companions.

2. 注目禮

併步站立，目視受禮者或向前平視，勿低頭彎腰，以表示對受禮者的恭敬、尊重。若表示對受禮者答諾或聆聽指教時，可微微點頭示意。

(2)「Zhumuli」(Greeting by looking)

Stand with feet close together. Look at the receiver, or just look straight ahead in courtesy and respect. Do not lower one's head or slouch. One may nod slightly to show acknowledgement and response to instruction.

附2　24式太極拳動作佈局路線圖

　　熟悉並掌握套路動作線路佈局變化十分重要，因為步法的變化，落腳之位置和方向，不僅影響套路演練的連貫性和美感，更重要的是它確保了每個招式的方向、位置和根基的穩固。

　　套路的練習目的不僅在於熟練動作，還包含了對肢體動作乃至招式之間的起承轉合的體悟，對於在攻防實踐中的運用招式有直接的影響，在增強表演觀賞效果方面也有重要的作用（見附圖）。

Appendix 2　Path Map of the 24-form Taiji Quan Movements

　　It is important to understand the path of the TaiJi forms. The location, the direction, and the translation between the steps have a great impact on the coherence of the whole form.

　　More important, the path provides a solid foundation for each movement. When practising, one should not only be familiar with the movements, but also understand the connection between the movements, which is more important when applying to attacking and defending (see the figure on Page 72).

151

24式太極拳 學與練

預備式 → 起式 → 左右野馬分鬃 → 白鶴亮翅 → 左右摟膝拗步 → 手揮琵琶 → 左右倒捲肱 → 左攬雀尾 → 右攬雀尾 → 單鞭 → 雲手 → 單鞭 → 高探馬 → 右蹬腳 → 雙峰貫耳 → 轉身左蹬腳 → 左下勢獨立 → 右下勢獨立 → 右穿梭 左穿梭 → 海底針 → 閃通臂 → 轉身搬攔捶 → 如封似閉 → 十字手 → 收式

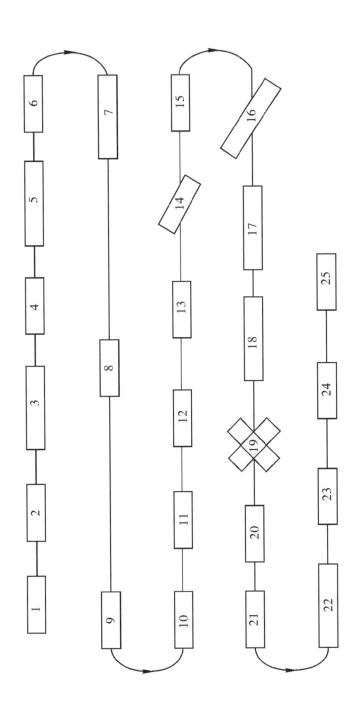

附2 24式太極拳動作佈局路線圖

153

1. Preparation

2. Opening

3. Splitting the Wild Horse's Mane – Left and Right

4. White Crane Spreading Wings

5. Brush Knees and Twist Steps – Left and Right

6. Playing the Pipa

7. Backward Steps and Swirling Arms – Left and Right

8. Grasp Bird's Tail – Left

9. Grasp Bird's Tail – Right

10. Single Whip

11. Cloud Hands

12. Single Whip

13. Patting a High Horse

14. Kicking with the Right Heel

15. Striking Ears with Both Fists

16. Turn and Kick with the Left Heel

17. Push Down and Stand on the Left Foot

18. Push Down and Stand on the Right Foot

19. Working with a Shuttle – Left and Right

20. Needle to the Bottom of the sea

21. Flashing the Arm

22. Turn, Deflect, Parry and Punch

23. Withdraw and Push

24. Crossing Hands

25. Closing

導引養生功

張廣德養生著作　　每冊定價350元

疏筋壯骨功
定價350元

導引保健功
定價350元

頤身九段錦
定價350元

九九還童功
定價350元

舒心平血功
定價350元

益氣養肺功
定價350元

養生太極扇
定價350元

養生太極棒
定價350元

導引養生形體詩韻
定價350元

四十九式經絡動功
定價350元

輕鬆學武術

二十四式太極拳
定價250元

四十二式太極拳
定價250元

八式十六式太極拳
定價250元

三十二式太極劍
定價250元

四十二式太極劍
定價250元

二十八式木蘭拳
定價250元

三十八式木蘭扇
定價250元

四十八式太極劍
定價250元

分解教學二十四式 簡化太極拳
定價280元

觀賞實用分解教學四十式 楊式太極拳
定價330元

太極跤

太極防身術
定價300元

擒拿術
定價280元

中國式摔角
定價350元

彩色圖解太極武術

定價220元

定價220元

定價220元

定價220元

定價350元

定價350元

定價350元

定價350元

定價350元

定價350元

定價350元

定價350元

定價350元

定價220元

定價220元

定價220元

定價350元

定價220元

定價350元

定價350元

定價220元

定價220元

定價220元

養生保健　古今養生保健法 強身健體增加身體免疫力

醫療養生氣功
定價250元

中國氣功圖譜
定價250元

少林醫療氣功精粹
定價250元

龍形實用氣功
定價220元

魚戲省視強身氣功
定價220元

道家玄北氣功
定價200元

仙家秘傳袪病功
定價160元

少林十大強身功
定價180元

中國自控氣功
定價250元

醫療防癌氣功
定價250元

醫療強身氣功
定價250元

醫療點穴氣功
定價250元

中國八卦如意功
定價180元

正宗馬禮堂養氣功
定價420元

道家筋經內丹功
定價300元

三元開慧功
定價250元

防癌治癌新氣功
定價180元

道定與佛家氣功修煉
定價200元

顛倒之術
定價360元

簡明氣功辭典
定價360元

八卦三合功
定價230元

朱砂掌健身養生功
定價250元

抗老功
定價230元

意氣按穴排濁自療法
定價250元

健身袪病小功法
定價200元

張氏太極混元功
定價250元

中國少林禪密功
定價200元

郭林新氣功
定價400元

太極
定價280元

現代原始氣功
定價400元

開脈太極
定價300元

養生保健大步功
定價300元

太極內功養生法
定價180元

無極養生氣功
定價200元

小周天健康法
定價200元

易筋經
定價350元

洗髓經
定價400元

精功易筋經
定價200元

武當熊門七心活氣功
定價280元

手杖健身法
定價200元

養生導引術
定價180元

養生長壽功
定價200元

太極拳內功養生心法
定價280元

意拳
定價280元

靜坐要訣
定價200元

太極武術教學光碟

太極功夫扇
五十二式太極扇
演示：李德印 等
(2VCD)中國

夕陽美太極功夫扇
五十六式太極扇
演示：李德印 等
(2VCD)中國

陳氏太極拳及其技擊法
演示：馬虹(10VCD)中國
陳氏太極拳勁道釋秘
拆拳講勁
演示：馬虹(8DVD)中國
推手技巧及功力訓練
演示：馬虹(4VCD)中國

陳氏太極拳新架一路
演示：陳正雷(1DVD)中國
陳氏太極拳新架二路
演示：陳正雷(1DVD)中國
陳氏太極拳老架一路
演示：陳正雷(1DVD)中國

陳氏太極拳老架二路
演示：陳正雷(1DVD)中國
陳氏太極推手
演示：陳正雷(1DVD)中國
陳氏太極單刀・雙刀
演示：陳正雷(1DVD)中國

郭林新氣功
(8DVD)中國

本公司還有其他武術光碟
歡迎來電詢問或至網站查詢
電話：02-28236031
網址：www.dah-jaan.com.tw

原版教學光碟

歡迎至本公司購買書籍

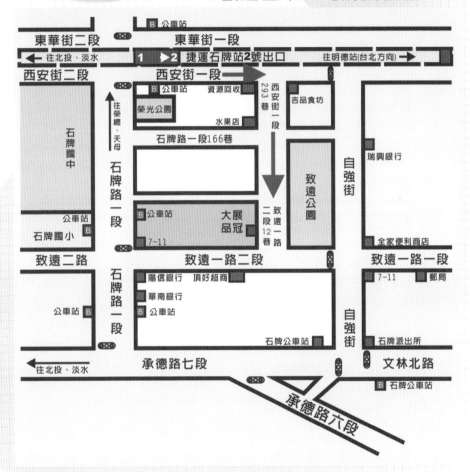

建議路線

1. 搭乘捷運‧公車

　　淡水線石牌站下車，由石牌捷運站2號出口出站(出站後靠右邊)，沿著捷運高架往台北方向走(往明德站方向)，其街名為西安街，約走100公尺(勿超過紅綠燈)，由西安街一段293巷進來(巷口有一公車站牌，站名為自強街口)，本公司位於致遠公園對面。搭公車者請於石牌站(石牌派出所)下車，走進自強街，遇致遠路口左轉，右手邊第一條巷子即為本社位置。

2. 自行開車或騎車

　　由承德路接石牌路，看到陽信銀行右轉，此條即為致遠一路二段，在遇到自強街(紅綠燈)前的巷子(致遠公園)左轉，即可看到本公司招牌。

國家圖書館出版品預行編目資料

24式太極拳學與練 ／ 李壽堂 編著
——初版，——臺北市，大展，2014〔民103.05〕
面；21公分 ——（中英文對照武學；1）
ISBN 978－986－346－017－6（平裝；附影音光碟）

1. 太極拳

528.972 103004224

24式太極拳學與練 附 VCD

編　　著／李壽堂
校　　訂／張連友
責任編輯／王躍平　　張東黎
發 行 人／蔡森明
出 版 者／大展出版社有限公司
社　　址／台北市北投區（石牌）致遠一路2段12巷1號
電　　話／（02）28236031・28236033・28233123
傳　　眞／（02）28272069
郵政劃撥／01669551
網　　址／www.dah-jaan.com.tw
E－mail／service@dah-jaan.com.tw
登 記 證／局版臺業字第2171號
承 印 者／傳興印刷有限公司
裝　　訂／承安裝訂有限公司
排 版 者／弘益電腦排版有限公司
授 權 者／山西科學技術出版社
初版1刷／2014年（民103年）5月

定　價／280元

●本書若有破損、缺頁請寄回本社更換●

大展好書　好書大展
品嘗好書　冠群可期